There is HOPE

HOW *GRACE* CAN *TRANSFORM* YOUR LIFE

13 Leaders on Grace & Forgiveness

There is Hope
How Grace can Transform your Life

Published by: Main Street Books

Cover & Interior Design: Linda Lanning

ISBN: 978 - 0 - 9890173 - 9 - 8

Printed in USA by The Print Steward.

There is
HOPE

HOW *GRACE*
CAN *TRANSFORM*
YOUR LIFE

M S B
MAIN STREET BOOKS

13 Leaders on Grace & Forgiveness

Table of Contents

CHAPTER 1
The Power of
Transformational Grace

Pastor Terry Bailey
TENNESSEE ASSEMBLIES OF GOD MINISTRY NETWORK

Bless the Lord, O my soul; And all that is within me, bless His holy name! Bless the Lord, O my soul, and forget not all His benefits (Psalm 103:1-2).

Jesus Christ can bring transformational change to your life through grace and forgiveness. You may look at the circumstances of your life and think to yourself that real change is not ever going to happen, but let me assure you that all things are possible with God. In my own life, God gave me the grace to forgive my dad for physical abuse. His abusive behavior almost resulted in his murder. Murder by whom? Me.

Growing up, my home life was very dysfunctional. My dad would physically abuse my mother and us kids. It wasn't an everyday occurrence but any abuse is never appropriate, whether the abuse is emotional, physical, or sexual. Dad never finished the eighth grade so he became stuck in a cycle of poverty which added to his frustrations with himself and others. He could be the nicest person you would ever want to meet, but his anger and rage could also explode the next moment. Abuse is about power and control. Not having grace and forgiveness operational within, retaliation becomes one of the ways to react when frustrated with life. Without the proper relationship skills to handle the hurts and disappointments of life, many people retaliate when things do not go their way. Hitting, slapping, yelling, name calling, throwing things, demeaning comments, shoving, bullying, and intimidation are different ways that people abuse others.

Without grace and forgiveness, those who have been abused are very likely to become abusers themselves. Just because someone has hurt you does not give you the right to hurt someone in return. Children and young people in abusive families become confused and do not know what to do. Searching for love and acceptance, they become vulnerable and fall prey to other abusers. Abuse becomes a terrible cycle that is passed from one generation to the next. It must be broken, but how? In my case, not knowing what to do nearly led to my murdering my dad.

My decision to almost murder my dad did not happen overnight. It came after hearing him cursing at and physically abusing my mother over a long period of time. Finally, after one horrific occurrence of his abuse, I reached the place where I decided that I needed to do something so he could not hurt her anymore. I told him not to ever touch my mother again and he cursed me out and hit me too. My decision became final in my mind. I decided that the next time my dad abused my mother, I would take my baseball bat and beat him to death. I would hit him in the head as hard as I could swing and knock him out. Then I would proceed to continue hitting him until there was no life left in his body. The plan was simple. It would be a brutal death but it would finally stop his abuse. What I did not realize was that his abuse would be passed on and I would become an abuser by murdering him. The cycle had to be broken.

As I contemplated his murder one night, I felt the prompting of the Holy Spirit speaking into my heart. The Holy Spirit's prompting was to forgive my dad for his abusive behavior. It was a tough moment of being confronted of my selfish plan to deal with our family's dysfunction by becoming an abuser myself. Because of my pain and my anger, I did not know how to truly forgive. After a struggle with my will, I responded by releasing my dad into God's hands and surrendered everything to allow God to work things out in His own way. That evening in my bed, as I cried out to God and let go of every bit of my hurt and pain, He gave me the grace to forgive my dad. My plan to murder my dad melted away as God's grace flooded my heart with forgiveness toward my dad. My act of forgiveness set me free, but did not immediately change my dad's abusive behavior. It would be several more years before my dad dedicated his life to Christ. Even as a Christian, my dad would sometimes relapse, but God would continue to give me the grace to forgive.

God's grace and forgiveness can be extended to every area of your life. Psalm 103 is one of my favorite chapters that demonstrates the power of God's grace and forgiveness. Read and meditate carefully upon these powerful words.

Bless the Lord, O my soul; And all that is within me, bless His holy name! Bless the Lord, O my soul, And forget not all His benefits: Who forgives all your iniquities, Who heals all your diseases, Who redeems your life from destruction, Who crowns you with lovingkindness and tender mercies, Who satisfies your mouth with good things, So that your youth is renewed like the eagle's. The Lord executes righteousness And justice for all who are oppressed. He made known His ways to Moses, His acts to the children of Israel. The Lord is merciful and gracious, Slow to anger, and abounding in mercy. He will not always strive with us, Nor will He keep His anger forever. He has not dealt with us according to our sins, Nor punished us according to our iniquities. For as the heavens are high above the earth, So great is His mercy toward those who fear Him; As far as the east is from the west, So far has He removed our transgressions from us. As a father pities his children, So the Lord pities those who fear Him. For He knows our frame; He remembers that we are dust. As for man, his days are like grass; As a flower of the field, so he flourishes. For the wind passes over it, and it is gone,

And its place remembers it no more. But the mercy of the Lord is from everlasting to everlasting On those who fear Him, And His righteousness to children's children, To such as keep His covenant, And to those who remember His commandments to do them. The Lord has established His throne in heaven, And His kingdom rules over all. Bless the Lord, you His angels, Who excel in strength, who do His word, Heeding the voice of His word. Bless the Lord, all you His hosts, You ministers of His, who do His pleasure. Bless the Lord, all His works, In all places of His dominion. Bless the Lord, O my soul!

Transformational change can happen in your life. Freddy Wicker would pass by Northside Assembly of God located on New Berlin Road in Jacksonville, Florida many times before he finally discovered God's grace and forgiveness at that incredible life-giving church. Freddy loved his rock and roll music. He even had his own rock band and following of music-loving fans. They all adored Freddy. Life was a big party consisting of rock music, drugs, sex, and hanging out with friends. However, Freddy came to realize that his life was empty and that he was destroying himself with his bad choices. I cannot remember how Freddy ended up at Northside Assembly, but one day he came through the doors of that church. All the young people present knew exactly who Freddy was when he walked in. As Freddy sat there and listened to Pastor Charles Lenn preach the Word of God, the Holy Spirit convicted Freddy of his sin and Freddy surrendered his life to Jesus Christ and became a Christian. When Freddy got saved, his whole entourage of friends got saved too.

God's grace and forgiveness transformed Freddy and his friends. The days of Freddy Wicker and his friends' worldly partying were over, and now they began partying for Jesus. Freddy still loved his music, and the louder the better. As Freddy's youth pastor, I told Freddy that he could keep his long hair and could now play his music for Jesus. Freddy loved that idea, so his rock band became a Christian rock band. When Freddy's band would have concerts for our Cornerstone youth services on Tuesday nights, young people would come from everywhere simply to hear Freddy's band play their music for Jesus. It was loud, so loud

I could hardly hear myself think, but young people were discovering God's grace and forgiveness through the music. Freddy asked me if his band could practice at the church, preparing for their concert at Cornerstone, and we obliged. Practices were so loud that we could easily hear their music sitting within our house next door. We replaced several tables they broke when they jumped from them and speakers they bursted, but it was all worthwhile because the lives of young adults were being transformed by God's grace and forgiveness.

God's grace and forgiveness are yours through Jesus Christ. God wants to forgive you of all your sins, to heal all your diseases, to redeem your life from destruction, to crown you with lovingkindness and tender mercies, to satisfy you with good things, and to renew your youth like the eagle's. How does God provide all those amazing benefits to you? Let's examine Psalm 103:3-5 more closely.

God forgives all your sins (Psalm 103:3). No matter what you have done, your sins can be forgiven. Despite your failures, God can forgive you and free you to start again. Your guilt and shame can be removed. Look at what the Lord says about grace and forgiveness, "Come now, and let us reason together. Though your sins are like scarlet, they shall be as white as snow; though they are red like crimson, they shall be as wool" (Isaiah 1:18). Jesus Christ took your place upon the cross and died for your sins. He shed His blood so you could be completely cleansed. Isaiah wrote, "All we like sheep have gone astray; we have turned, every one, to his own way; and the Lord has laid on Him the iniquity of us all" (Isaiah 53:6). The words of John 3:16 are just as true today as the time I first heard Pastor Joe Dee Kelly preach it when I was six years old: "For God so loved the world that He gave His only begotten Son, that whoever believes in Him should not perish but have everlasting life." The Bible also teaches, "If we confess our sins, He is faithful and just to forgive us our sins and to cleanse us from all un-righteousness" (1 John 1:9). You may feel like you cannot be forgiven, but I assure you that His grace is exactly what you need.

God heals all your diseases (Psalm 103:3). Jesus Christ not only died on the cross for your sins, but was beaten with stripes so that you could receive healing. The Bible says, "But He was wounded for our transgressions, He was bruised for our iniquities; The chastisement for our peace was upon Him, And by His stripes we are healed" (Isaiah 53:5). Have faith in God, not only saving faith but also faith for healing of your body, mind, and spirit. Emotional healing is available to you for depression, anxiety, fear, bitterness, and even bad attitudes. The book of James teaches, "Is anyone among you sick? Let him call for the elders of the church, and let them pray over him, anointing him with oil in the name of the Lord. And the prayer of faith will save the sick, and the Lord will raise him up. And if he has committed sins, he will be forgiven" (James 5:14-15).

God redeems your life from destruction (Psalm 103:4). As a Christian, you have a divine protection plan operating in your life. God often steps in and rescues you in times of danger. Only heaven will reveal the many times your life and your loved ones were protected by angels unaware. The Psalmist wrote:

Surely He shall deliver you from the snare of the fowler and from the perilous pestilence. He shall cover you with His feathers, and under His wings you shall take refuge; His truth shall be your shield and buckler. You shall not be afraid of the terror by night, Nor of the arrow that flies by day, Nor of the pestilence that walks in darkness, Nor of the destruction that lays waste at noonday...For He shall give His angels charge over you, To keep you in all your ways. In their hands they shall bear you up, lest you dash your foot against a stone (Psalm 91:3-6, 11-12).

There is no pit too deep for God's deliverance. God crowns you with lovingkindness and tender mercies (Psalm 103:4). God's loving kindness and tender mercies are greater than you could ever imagine. God is for you, not against you. As you "delight yourself also in the Lord, He shall give you the desires of your heart. Commit your way to the Lord, Trust also in Him, And He shall bring it to pass" (Psalm 37:4-5). God's grace gives to you that which you could never deserve, and God's mercy withholds from you that which you actually deserve. His loving kindness and tender mercies are priceless.

God satisfies you with good things (Psalm 103:5). Nobody or nothing will ever satisfy you like God does. The Psalmist wrote, "You will show me the path of life; In Your presence is fullness of joy; At Your right hand are pleasures forevermore" (Psalm 16:11). Jesus taught, "But seek the kingdom of God, and all these things shall be added to you. Do not fear, little flock, for it is your Father's good pleasure to give you the kingdom" (Luke 11:31-32). Charles Spurgeon once said, "If there were an ant at the door of your granary begging for help, it wouldn't ruin you to give him a grain of your wheat. You are but a tiny insect at the door of God's all-sufficiency." God will always be your source of supply for every need.

God renews your youth like the eagle's (Psalm 103:5). As one grows older, you long for the times when your physical energy was renewed. You start slowing down and your strength does not endure as long as it once did. God gives a spiritual renewal as you wait in His presence that far exceeds physical stamina. Isaiah wrote, "He gives power to the weak, And to those who have no might He increases strength. Even the youths shall faint and be weary, And the young men shall utterly fall, But those who wait on the Lord shall renew their strength; They shall mount up with wings like eagles, They shall run and not be weary, They shall walk and not faint" (Isaiah 40:29-31). As you wait on the Lord, your strength will be renewed like an eagle.

Maury Davis, Senior Pastor at Cornerstone Nashville, has perhaps the greatest testimony of grace and forgiveness that I have ever personally known. In a recent powerful sermon on October 22, 2017 about The Blood, Pastor Maury preached, "I don't know if it is personal to you or not but the blood of Jesus is personal to me because in 1975, sitting in a cell, demon possessed, my hands are covered in guilt and shame and blood. I had done the most horrible thing you could do to a another human being and at the end of that day, there's no hope for me. The psychiatrists had said that we can't help him. The lawyer said we can't help him. And someone introduced me to Jesus Christ and Jesus said give me your mind and I am going to put the blood on your mind. And give me your heart and I am going to put the blood on your heart. And give me your hands. You can't wash them but I can wash them as if they had never been dirty. You'll no longer do harm, you'll lay hands on the sick and they will recover. I am going to put some blood on you that will change your destiny. Jesus Christ wants to put the blood in areas of your life where only the blood can fix your life."

No matter the circumstances of your life, God's grace and forgiveness through Jesus Christ is available to you. Your life can be transformed. Real change can happen. God abounds in mercy, willing to withhold what you actually deserve for your sins. If you will repent of your sins, God will remove your transgressions as far as the east is from the west. God knows that you are merely human with frailties and faults; however, His mercy is from everlasting to everlasting. When you repent of your sins, God will remember your sins no more. Receive God's grace and forgiveness.

TERRY BAILEY *serves as the District Superintendent of the Tennessee Assemblies of God Ministry Network in Nashville, Tennessee.*

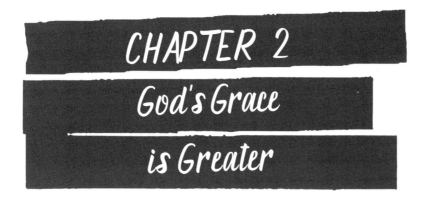

CHAPTER 2
God's Grace
is Greater

Gene Garcia
MEMPHIS ADULT TEEN CHALLENGE

And you hath he quickened, who were dead in trespasses and sins; Wherein in time past ye walked according to the course of this world, according to the prince of the power of the air, the spirit that now worketh in the children of disobedience: For by grace are ye saved through faith; and that not of yourselves: it is the gift of God: Not of works, lest any man should boast (Ephesians 2:1-2, 8-9).

God has forgiven me so very much. I was one of the most unforgiving, unloving, rude, crude, obnoxious, nasty attitude, self-centered, money loving, and inconsiderate person you probably would have ever met in your lifetime; but because of His Grace I am not 6 feet under or locked up in prison forever, where I should have been, instead of here writing this to you. Thank God by His grace, I am now approximately four years into my walk with the Lord.

And he said unto me, my grace is sufficient for thee: for my strength is made perfect in weakness. Most gladly therefore will I rather glory in my infirmities, that the power of Christ may rest upon me. Therefore I take pleasure in infirmities, in reproaches, in necessities, in persecutions, in distresses for Christ's sake: for when I am weak, then am I strong (2 Corinthians 12:9-10).

This is what happened with the Apostle Paul. If we allow the Lord He can do the same for us because his goal is Christ in us, the hope of glory.

If it wasn't for Jesus leading me to Teen Challenge, once again I would not be here writing this to you. Teen Challenge and the people in it have meant so much to me in my walk with the Lord. Thank God for Teen Challenge. I would highly recommend it to those who are looking for a rehabilitation center. I had taken enough different types of drugs in my life time to kill a small elephant! I laugh now, but at the time it was no laughing matter, it wasn't funny at all. I had many heart attacks, seizures, and over doses that the Lord miraculously saved me from. One day, I finally came to a crossroad where I had to make a decision that would affect me for eternity. My choices were life and follow Christ, or death and eternal damnation. Matthew 6:24 says, "No man can serve two masters: for either he will hate the one, and love the other; or else he will hold to the one, and despise the other. Ye cannot serve God and mammon."

I grew up at the Jersey Shore. There was a hotel that I used to drive past, and at that time I would say the people in the car, look at that place, you couldn't pay me to live there. This place was the lowest of the lows on the Shore. My mentor told me in the past I was pride personified. In my pride I viewed the people that lived there as outcasts, losers, and worthless individuals who put themselves there and no one should feel bad for them, or have compassion for them. As a matter of fact, I don't even think compassion was a word in my vocabulary back then. I said to myself, that I would never end up like those people, or in a place like that. I said that would never be me, but after many years of drug and alcohol use, very sinful living, ending up without a home, being on the streets, having no place to go, I ended up there. It didn't happen right away, because once again in my pride, when I viewed my life, I would think at times, I got this, but I was so sadly mistaken.

Since a very young age I was taught by words, actions, and deeds from people that were in my life, that life should be centered on getting money and nothing else. After that, everything else would fall into place. Money, and the things it bought, would make me happy, complete and give me peace, so I went about my life doing this. I had fancy cars all done up that were mine, jewelry, a beautiful fiancé, significant money saved up. I went on nice trips and I was partnered with a successful company, which I made more in one month at times than what some people make in a year. Yet, despite having money and material things I was still miserable, lonely empty. I had no peace. Please don't misunderstand what I'm trying to say here, it is nice to have money and nice things, but just don't let money and nice things have you like I did. I looked to the money as if it was my god and my savior. My identity was in what I had and what people thought of me. I had to support myself and my many addictions. In turn when all the money, stuff and people were gone, so was my identity and I felt worthless. 1 Timothy 6:10 (KJV) "For the love of money is the root **of all evil: which while some coveted after, they have erred from the faith, and pierced themselves through with many sorrows."** You see I tried to get peace from all that stuff, money and people, but it was a false peace that left me in pieces. **John 14:27 KJV "Peace I leave with you, my peace I give unto you: not as the world giveth, give I unto you. Let not your heart be troubled, neither let it be afraid."** You see I was a fan of Jesus, not a follower. The thought that Jesus could do things for me was great, but the thought of me laying it all down for him was not even a consideration. Now nothing really was happening in my life. As a matter of fact, it was just the same thing repeatedly, just with different people and different places. I was like a gerbil in a cage going around and around trapped not getting anywhere good.

Back to what happened in the hotel. My addiction finally led me to living in this same hotel that I said that I would never ever go to. Now here I am at this place of disgrace feeling as if I had no grace about to fall on my face. Pacing back and forth in this hotel thinking to myself *I am a junkie*; something I never wanted to be or thought I could be. In my life I couldn't just be myself, <u>I always had to be what the world told me I needed to be, to feel loved.</u> Now keep in mind there was a time where I would do multiple drugs at once, and at this point in this room I was addicted to nicotine, opioids which included my prescription medications at the time roxycodone 30mg pills, Adderall and Xanax. Now in this room at this time all I had on me was my prescription of Xanax and Adderall on me. I was pacing in this room I start talking to myself saying, *I don't know what to do with myself, I don't know what to do with myself.* As I was doing that, I thought about some of the promises of God I had heard growing up. I remembered what a pastor told me. He said, "If you get serious with God He will get serious with you." As that hit me, I threw my hands up looking at the ceiling saying to God, "Alright you win that's it." Then I fell to my knees in a prostate position saying, "I surrender all!" Let thy kingdom, thy will be done, crying my eyes out meaning everything I said with every part of me and all my heart. <u>You see everything that I was seeking love from and thought it would set me free from the stress and problems of this world was holding me captive and had me in a prison that I couldn't set myself free from.</u> I tried many things to get off all the drugs. I tried NA, suboxone, methadone, getting committed to a hospital, quitting cold turkey on my own strength, trying to cover up withdraw symptoms with other drugs and alcohol which only prolonged the use of opioids which made the addiction worse. Nothing was working, BUT **JESUS**. I tried everything. If you could name it more than likely I tried it. Then I figured I had tried everything, let me try **JESUS**.

Now that night the enemy tried to stake claim on what he thought was his (me). The spiritual warfare for my soul began. Now at this time, I was withdrawing from everything I was on, but I had made up my mind also to follow Jesus no matter the cost, and so I decided to read the Bible. When I was trying to read the Bible, everything got blurred and the words on the page kept on shifting from left to right. When I was trying to read the Bible, I heard a voice that I thought was God in the room saying, thou shall not covet, thou shall not have any Gods before me, thou shall not have any graven images before me. All my windows were shut and I didn't have any air-conditioning on, and suddenly a rushing wind came in the room and knocked off the wall a wooden cross I had hanging up. I went and took the broken piece and hung it back up, but the rushing wind came again and knocked it down. I fell to my knees saying, "I'm sorry." About ten minutes later I went back into my bed. Then I heard a real evil voice say to me, *you don't look good*, then I heard other evil voices in the room saying master. I remember being petrified. I tried reading the Bible again but it wasn't making sense to me. Then the voice said to me if I follow the Lord, my mom and pastor would die in a certain amount of days. Suddenly something grabbed my throat and started to choke me as it said *you don't even know His name*. As I was getting choked, with one last gasp of air that I was able to get out, I said **JESUS**. Then whatever was choking me stopped, and at this point, freaking out I got up, but consumed by fear, wouldn't go outside, and stayed in the room. The room started to shift back and forth. I turned on TV to Christian channel trying to calm down, but as I watched the Pastor at the pulpit on the TV, *he said let's go to the beach and have some beer*. Now at this point beyond petrified not wanting to take anything. Still having my prescription medication at the time Xanax and Adderall in my pocket. I went back to the bed and tried to fall asleep again but couldn't. Then the left side of my chest got super tight. I felt a great pain, a numbness and a tingling wrapped all in one, shot down my left arm into my hands and my fingers. Then I heard that super evil voice say to me, *not being able to sleep is a curse, take something to make it go away*. Suddenly, I felt something moving around in my pocket. I went into that pocket where I felt that and took the bottle with the Xanax out of it, and as I did that, I notice one pill at a time like the way popcorn pops was rising to top of bottle very slowly and falling back down, and as one fell, another one raised up hitting the top of the inside of the cap and so got up from bed, threw both prescriptions on the shelf where the TV was, and walked away from them. I went back into room tried to fall asleep but couldn't, and then, suddenly getting bold, I jumped up at the window saying to the devil *show me your worse and I will show you mine*. I went back into bed and as I laid there threw my hands up praising the Lord in full surrender. Shortly after that there was two men with a flash light looking into my window. Still

I wouldn't put my hands down. Then I again I called out on the name of **JESUS. Psalm 50:15 KJV "And call upon me in the day of trouble: I will deliver thee, and thou shalt glorify me."** It felt like I had my arms and hands up in that surrender position for hours. I woke up the next day not remembering when or how I fell asleep. Now there was a fragrance, presence and peace in the room no words could describe. I had my eyes opened and something fell from my eyes and dissipated into the air. This is when I knew I truly became born again. **Isaiah 43:19 KJV "Behold, I will do a new thing; now it shall spring forth; shall ye not know it? I will even make a way in the wilderness, and rivers in the desert."**

At this point of was truly set free from my drug addictions. **John 8:36 KJV "If the Son therefore shall make you free, ye shall be free indeed."**

I tried so hard to be perfect because of all my insecurities, and as I was trying to be perfect one day, my mentor said to me, your perfection is causing your imperfection. Now I know that the only thing perfect in me is the Christ within me. All I must do now is yield to him, submit to him and He will do the work.

I have learned so much from every Teen Challenge that I have been a part of. I went through the program itself at Teen Challenge New Jersey. After that I went to Brooklyn Teen Challenge where I attended their School of Ministry. I have learned the most from the Adult and Teen Challenge of Memphis which I currently serve on staff. Presently I am going to be receiving my credentials to be a minister through the Assemblies of God. For one who was helpless, hopeless, and useless, the Father, in His love and forgiveness, has caused me to be hopeful, useful and helpful in His service. Hallelujah!

GENE GARCIA serves as a campus staff member at Memphis Adult Teen Challenge in Memphis, Tennessee. Gene has completed the first level of the ministerial credential process with the AG and is now a certified minister with them.

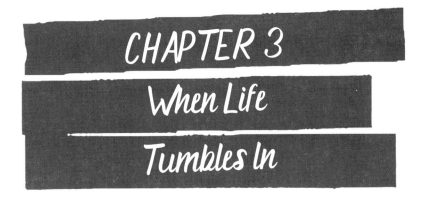

CHAPTER 3
When Life
Tumbles In

Reverend Daniel Johnson
ASSEMBLIES OF GOD EVANGELIST

Out of nowhere it comes. No matter how hard one tries to build a good life, craft a satisfying career, develop comfortable relationships, something will inevitably ruin it. It's not a matter of *if* but when. "Trouble is not an interruption in life," Bruce Barton wrote, "it's the stuff of which life is made." And the Word of God declares, "Man is born to trouble as the sparks fly upward." It's written into the warp and woof of the human condition, and none are exempt. You don't live long until the landscape of human life becomes cluttered with small discomforts and sometimes large tragedies. We struggle with temptation and sin; experience accident and injury. We wrestle with our mortality, battle a variety of illnesses, and finally we die.

It's not a matter of if a fiery trial or bitter disappointment might spoil an otherwise perfect day, it's a matter of when. But another question arises: Why? How do you make sense of it all? Is life simply random? Is this earthly journey some kind of joke? Is there a scheme, some kind of design to human existence, and if so, is there a designer? Stephen Hawking, the brilliant scientist, didn't think so. "We are such insignificant creatures," he writes, "on a minor planet of a very average star at the outer suburbs of a hundred, thousand, million galaxies, so it is very difficult to believe in a God who would care for us or even notice our existence."

If there is a God, where is He when it hurts? Why is He silent? It cannot be denied that the greatest challenge to the Christian faith is the existence of evil, the problem of suffering. If God is benevolent and omnipotent, why do the righteous suffer? Why do bad things happen to good people? For Ted Turner, who gave us CNN, God's "silence" was inexcusable. Early in his life his sister became ill. Turner said that he prayed for her healing 30 minutes a day for five years, but his sister died. "If there is a God," Turner concluded, "he has checked out. I don't want anything more to do with him."

A Jewish proverb says, "If God lived on earth, people would break His windows." An Arab proverb is not much better: "If you meet a blind man on the road, kick him; why should you be kinder than God?" And George P. Elliot wrote, "What I found as wrong was so vast, there could be no one worth blaming for it but God."

And why does God sometimes seem most remote while one is walking most closely with Him: Look at John the Baptist, the great prophet and revival preacher. The people thronged his message and responded to the waters of baptism. He nearly brought the whole nation to its knees, but now he's in a prison cell, his obedience having brought him to the place of death. And the questions arise: Why this, why now? And he sends a message to Jesus, "Art thou He that should come, or do we look for another?"

Jesus sent word back to the imprisoned preacher, "Go and tell John the things you hear and see: the blind see and the lame walk; the lepers are cleansed and the deaf hear; the dead are raised up and the poor have the Gospel preached to them. And blessed is he who is not offended in Me" (Matthew 11:4-6).

GOD IS GOOD

There are 300 questions in the Book of Job and most of them are never answered, and the unanswered questions haunt us throughout life. Someone once wrote Billy Graham and asked, "I've never understood something about God. If God is supposed to be good, where did evil come from?" C.S. Lewis was a confirmed bachelor until his mid-fifties when he married an American poet, Joy Davidman Gresham. They lived together four exquisite years and, although stricken with cancer before their marriage, her death left Lewis totally devastated. *A Grief Observed* records the thoughts and pain of those days. A poignant line appears early in the small volume: "Meanwhile, where is God?"

But bringing God into the equation raises other questions. Who is God, and what kind of God is He? A.W. Tozer wrote, "What comes into your mind when you think about God is the most important thing about you." The Christian faith asserts with confidence that God is good. There is a God and He is good. The enemy induced Eve to question God's essential goodness and we've been doing it ever since. We blame Him for accidents, misfortune, tragedies. Whatever our theological persuasions and however difficult life's problems may be, let us not malign God. It is the character of a thief to steal, to kill, to destroy. It is the nature of God to forgive, to help, to restore. Wherever the Gospel goes, the lot of man improves. It is God's business to save and to help, to lift up. God does not cause the tragedy and terror that stalk the earth. He may allow it and employ it for our good; but He does not cause it, nor is it His will.

Richard Halverson, former Senate chaplain, said:

It may be difficult to explain how a God of love could allow the terrible agony, suffering, and tragedy in the world, but it is infinitely more difficult to explain these facts of life and leave God out of the picture. The intention, character, and love of God were never more accurately depicted than on that day long ago when a cross was planted on a hill outside the walls of Jerusalem. There, by a great highway, the Savior was crucified. There God was in Christ reconciling the world to Himself. On that cross, as through His earthly ministry, Jesus set Himself against sin, disease, poverty, fear, and death. He is still against them.

It is very interesting that Jesus made no attempt to answer some questions, but did something better in demonstrating His love by what He did. N.T. Wright wrote, "Jesus doesn't give an explanation for the pain and sorrow in our world. He comes where the pain is most acute and takes it upon Himself. He doesn't allow the problem of suffering to be the subject of a seminar. He allows evil to do its worst to Him; then exhausts it, drains its power and emerges with new life."

GOD IS ALL-KNOWING

The fact that God knows everything was a source of comfort to Oral and Evelyn Roberts when tragedy struck their lives. Early on a Saturday morning a friend knocked on the back door. He opened the newspaper and showed them the story of a plane crash. "We think it's Marshall and Rebecca," he said. Rebecca was the oldest of the four Roberts children and Marshall was her husband. Returning from a skiing trip in Colorado, they had crashed in a wheat field in Kansas. Another couple died as well.

The first concern was for the children, now orphaned. They immediately dressed and prepared to drive across town to where the children were being cared for. While they were driving, Oral Roberts said, "My first word was why, why has this happened to me? What have I done to deserve this? This is our oldest daughter, precious daughter and precious son-in-law. Why?" And then the Lord brought this to my heart, *God must know something about this we don't know.*"

Look at Job—he never knew what hit him, or why. He lived his entire life unaware of the drama going on in the heavens. The Bible says that Job was "the greatest of all the people in the East." He had great possessions; seven thousand sheep, three thousand camels, five hundred yoke of oxen, five hundred female donkeys, and a very large household.

He was a devout man, loyal husband, faithful father. He rose early in the morning to offer burnt offerings for his children. But there came a day when Satan presented himself before the Lord. He accused Job of serving God for gain. He charged him with "commercial faith"—*he's in this for what he can get out of it*. Satan maligned Job's character, his motives.

When given permission to try the poor man, Satan unleashed the forces of nature. Job lost his family, his possessions and his health – and he never knew what hit him. Job was unaware of the contest in heaven, but God knew – and Job trusted God.

GOD IS PURPOSEFUL

The purposes of suffering are clearly stated in the Word of God: "My brethren, count it all joy when you fall into various trials, knowing that the testing of your faith produces patience" (James 1:2, 3). "Beloved, do not think it strange concerning the fiery trial which is to try you, as though some strange thing happened to you; but rejoice to the extent that you partake of Christ's sufferings, that when His glory is revealed, you may also be glad with exceeding joy" (1 Peter 4:12, 13).

Development of character and growth in grace are often the result of positive response to pressure at some point in our lives. "Now no chastening seems to be joyful for the present, but painful." Paul writes, "Nevertheless, afterward it yields the peaceable fruit of righteousness to those who have been trained by it" (Hebrews 12:11).

Dr. Paul Tournier was a general practitioner in Geneva for nearly 50 years. Without special training and disdaining the title of psychiatrist, he came to develop the practice what he called "medicine of the person." Many patients, he came to believe, needed help going deeper than drugs or surgery. His keen insight is illustrated in one of his books when he speaks of the blessings of a deep loss: "The greater the grief, the greater the creative energy to which it gives rise."

Sometimes we are forced to grow, and "the whole purpose of life is to grow," Dr. Robert R. Carkhuff writes in his excellent book, *The Art of Helping*. "We are born with the potential to grow – no more – no less. From the moment we enter the world to the instant we exit this life, we experience opportunities for growth."

God permitted Job to suffer in order to silence Satan. Former pastor and prolific author Warren Wiersbe made a striking observation when he wrote: "By the way, have you ever stopped to consider that God paid a great price for you and me? Because he lost everything, and by his suffering proved Satan wrong, you and I don't have to lose everything. God can test us on a much smaller scale because the battle against Satan's lie has now been won by God."

Disappointment and pain have a way of weaning us away from this world. Joni Eareckson Tada writes in *A Step Further*: "Suffering gets us ready for heaven. How does it get us ready? It makes us want to go there. Broken necks, broken arms, broken bones, broken hearts – these things crush our illusions that earth can keep its promises. When we come to know that the hopes we cherished will never come true, that our loved one is gone from this life forever, that we will never be as pretty, popular, successful, or famous as we had once imagined, it lifts our sights. It moves our eyes from this world, which God knows could never satisfy us anyway, and sets them on the life to come. Heaven becomes our passion."

A friend and I agonized over a difficult situation. "When we get to heaven," I volunteered, "we'll ask the Lord about it."

"When we get to heaven, it won't make any difference," my friend replied.

In his little book, *Inward Ho,* Christopher Morely wrote, "I had a million questions to ask God; but when I met Him, they all fled my mind; and it didn't seem to matter."

Until that Day dawns and the shadows flee away, we might find comfort in the words of noted author, Phillip Yancey: "I am gaining gradually the confidence to believe in the present what will fully make sense only when seen from the future."

DANIEL E. JOHNSON serves as an evangelist with the Assemblies of God. A former pastor, he now devotes his time to research and writing on cultural issues. He and his wife are the parents of three children and reside in Memphis, Tennessee.

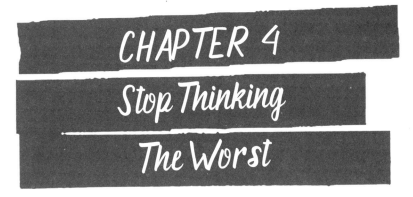

CHAPTER 4
Stop Thinking
The Worst

Dr. Thomas Lindberg
MEMPHIS FIRST ASSEMBLY

Let me ask you a question: When is the last time you felt everything in your life was going wrong? Was it last year? Last month? Or was it last week? Let's be honest, sometimes life can be more difficult than being fourteen months pregnant! But thank God for His amazing grace.

Now I've met people who say if you have real faith you'll never face a problem. They say you'll just bounce along in life from mountain top to mountain top. But I've got news for you: you cannot have mountains without valleys. If you doubt that, just travel to East Tennessee and check me out.

Let's back the calendar up 2,800 years and meet a man named Elijah. What a man! He was obedient, faithful and godly. But during a season of time, life got really rough for Elijah. At that point in his life, Elijah made a big mistake—a mistake I don't want you to make. Elijah began thinking the worst. Listen to him: "Elijah was afraid and fled for his life. He went to Beersheba, a town in Judah, and he left his servant there. Then he went on alone into the desert, traveling all day. He sat down under a solitary broom tree and prayed that he might die. "I have had enough, LORD," he said. "Take my life, for I am no better than my ancestors" (1 Kings 19:3-4 NLT).

What is Elijah doing? He's allowing his thoughts to run wild and he's thinking the worst. That can happen to the best of us. But it always spells trouble. How can you stop from thinking the worst? Four words that become principles can help you and they are all summed up in the word S.T.O.P.

S = Stir: Stir your spiritual memory.

Elijah had been threatened by Queen Jezebel and his thoughts began to run terribly wild. You know what Elijah should have done? He should have stirred his spiritual memory, reminding himself that God had miraculously fed him by the Brook Cherith, had supernaturally supplied food for a widow and him, had raised a boy from the dead through his prayers, and had sent fire from heaven on Mount Carmel. Elijah should have said something like this: "Yes, I'm in a mess. But I've been in a mess before and God brought me through all those times. I will trust Him again and I refuse to think the worst."

One major news network has labeled this year as "The Year Of Fear." Let me give you the Bible's definition of fear. Fear is that feeling that overwhelms you when you get your eyes off Jesus. Remember what the Bible tells you: "God has not given us a spirit of fear, but of power, love, and self-control" (2 Timothy 1.7).

In Psalm 40, David is in the pits of life (check out verse 1). What does David do? Does he start thinking the worst? No! Instead he says, "O LORD my God, you have done many miracles for us.

Your plans for us are too numerous to list. If I tried to recite all your wonderful deeds, I would never come to the end of them" (verse 5, NLT). In simple words, David stirred his spiritual memory and didn't let his thoughts go crazy.

I like the little couplet…

Yesterday God helped me,
Today He'll do the same.
How long will this continue?
Forever, praise His name.

Make that your own!

T = Talk: Talk to yourself.

The Bible says "We are not to be ignorant of Satan's devices" (2 Corinthians 2:11). Now listen, I know how the devil works. When problems crash into your life, Satan begins by exaggerating the problem. He blows them up and makes them seem much worse than they are. Next he blinds you to the promises of God (see Romans 8:28). You see, if the devil can shut your eyes to God's Word, he has stripped you of your greatest weapon. Last, the devil gets your mind racing and thinking the worst. How do you stop the black-winged dragon from the pit from causing you to fly into panic mode? You don't listen to him or yourself; you talk to yourself.

Years ago I discovered a lump on my neck. "What's that?" I thought. Now, the week before I had visited someone in the hospital who had a lump in their body that turned out to be cancer. Know what happened to me? I'm ashamed to admit that my mind began to race, I began thinking the worst, I convinced myself I was going to die from cancer, and I even began planning my funeral! (The lump turned out to be a knot in one of my muscles and disappeared in ten days.) You see, I fell into the same trap as Elijah. I began thinking the worst. You know what I learned way back then? Don't listen to yourself, but instead talk to yourself. And the best things to say are to quote Scripture.

Please don't doubt me. Learn to quote scripture out loud and watch it help you stop thinking the worst. Four of my favorite verses to quote are these:

"Be strong and courageous! Do not be afraid of them! The LORD

your God will go ahead of you. He will neither fail you nor forsake you" (Deuteronomy 31:6).

"But you, O LORD, are a shield around me, my glory, and the one who lifts my head high" (Psalm 3:3).

"O LORD, I will honor and praise your name, for you are my God. You do such wonderful things! You planned them long ago, and now you have accomplished them" (Isaiah 25:1).

"Don't be afraid, for I am with you. Do not be dismayed, for I am your God. I will strengthen you. I will help you. I will uphold you with my victorious right hand" (Isaiah 41:10).

You see, you have a choice when life turns rough. You can let the devil exaggerate your problem, let your mind run wild, and start thinking the worst, OR you can take God's Word and speak it out loud to yourself. Let me make a promise from experience: if you do the latter, it will be like drinking liquid power.

O = Opportunity: Instead of thinking the worst, look for an opportunity to open up in your future.

Consider Elijah. He thought his life was over. Do you want to know the truth? God was setting up an opportunity for Elijah. God wanted Elijah's attention so He could change Elijah's direction. You see, while Elijah was thinking the worst, God was planning the best. The prophet was yet to receive more divine revelation, anoint the next king, develop Elisha to be a mighty prophet, and ultimately go to heaven without dying in chariots of fire. God did a miracle for Elijah. You say, "I'm not sure I believe in miracles." Let me tell you something: you will when you need one!

Read the next sentence carefully: Life is 10% what happens to you and 90% how you respond to it. For example, the Apostle Paul was in prison. He wrote from jail to the Ephesian church and said, "I am a prisoner of Jesus Christ." Not a prisoner of the Roman government—a prisoner of Jesus Christ. Paul could have started to think the worst, but he looked for an opportunity during difficult times. And guess what? God gave him opportunities to witness for God.

In every Christian's life there is the natural and the supernatural. The natural is obviously you and the supernatural is clearly God. Don't you think it's time we stop living all of our life in the natural and start living more and thinking more in the supernatural?

P = Persist: Persist in your battle to stop thinking the worst.

I told you I know how the devil works. When you beat him once, do you think he gives up and retreats with his tail between his legs? Not on your life. He will attack you again and again and again. You need to be persistent in your fight against him. God's personal grace to you will give you the strength you need.

For example, imagine a June day. The mosquitoes are thick. One lands on your left arm. You swat at it and miss. What does that bug do? He moves to your right arm. Then to your leg. Then to your back. You must keep hitting at that mosquito until he leaves.

So it is with the devil. Get rid of the idea that being a follower of the Lord Jesus takes little effort, it's for the lazy, and a fight is never required. Listen, you will never be free from spiritual warfare, so you better learn to fight, and to fight well. Spiritual victory is not purchased at the cheapest price in the shortest time possible. God wants you to be persistent. And You Can Through Jesus Christ!

I know a lady who a few years ago went through a rough time, much like Elijah. God was faithful and brought her through. But during those days she wrote and clung to these words:

> *"The Lord may not have planned that this bad thing should overtake me, but He most certainly knew about it. Therefore, even though it were an attack from the enemy, by the time it reaches me it has the Lord's permission—*

therefore <u>ALL</u> <u>IS</u> <u>WELL</u>!"

I challenge you, stir up your spiritual memory. Talk to yourself instead of listening to yourself. Look for opportunities during difficult days. And persist in your fight against a devil who never takes a vacation. If you do, you'll like the results—I guarantee it.

THOMAS LINDBERG is the Lead Pastor of First Assembly Memphis. He has served on the Board of Adult & Teen Challenge of Memphis since 1996.

CHAPTER 5
Miracle
Whip

Pastor Craig McGee
VICTORY LIFE CHURCH

It was a chilly October evening in Memphis when I first began my journey serving as a pastor in a community full of poverty and despair, where hope was sparse.

This assignment was during a time in my life where I was young in age and full of many hopes and dreams, ready to win everyone to Christ! I believed that where sin abounds, grace abounds much, and God was ready to work miracles! I believed and taught that we are a miracle because of our salvation in Christ and a miracle for someone else by sharing Christ with others.

God directed me to start a bus route picking up children and adults to attend our Thursday night Bible Study. The Holy Spirit's anointing and protection was so strong as we walked in obedience, proclaiming God's love to our community. The bus route was a lifeline to so many. For me, as a young minister, it was just the beginning of being immersed in the power of the Holy Spirit, experiencing signs and wonders.

That cold and chilly fall night, while driving the bus filled with excitement, with kids joking and laughing, we had no idea what God was going to do that evening in the lives of those individuals. Even to this day I rejoice and shout that we serve a living God that works in miracles.

When we arrived at the church we broke up into age groups. On this particular evening I was teaching one of the small groups for adults. While heading back to the classrooms, one of the ladies in our church touched my arm and said, "Pastor, we've got to pray and believe in faith for Ms. Shawanna. Her ear hurts, she has a lump on her neck and she has spoken very little since she went to the doctor's office." When we got into our classroom, I could see that Ms. Shawanna was in pain as she was seated in the chair. I asked her if the class could pray for her.

She began to tell us the report from the doctor, that she had cancer and showed us the 1 ½ inch growth on the side of her neck. She needed a miracle because she did not have any money to pay for the medical treatment. You could see the fear on her face. The group in this class was new to Christianity, full of questions and faith. The whole hour of the class was spent reading the scripture out loud and proclaiming healing in the name of Jesus for Ms. Shawanna. In the natural, nothing happened to that growth that we could see. In the supernatural, what the group proclaimed, happened. Ms. Shawanna went home believing in faith that she would be healed.

Three days later, our Sunday bus route picked up Ms. Shawanna. She was happy and full of joy, crying as she was walking though the church doors holding a small Miracle Whip jar in her hands right before worship service. I was on the front row worshipping to the first song, service had already begun. I could hear people talking loudly rather than worshipping to the song. I could tell something was going on, I turned around and Ms. Shawanna was walking down the aisle with a Miracle Whip jar in her hand. She said loudly, "God Healed me and I got the proof." Immediately, I began to weep!

She continued with a loud voice, "The growth fell off in the middle of the night while I was sleeping and I placed it in the Miracle Whip jar. I received my miracle and I got proof, my God answers prayers!"

This miracle took place 2002 years later because Jesus died and arose 3 days later.

Picture this with me today! Jesus was falsely accused, placed on trial, was beaten and whipped and sent to death for the punishment of our sins. He was given a cross to carry and led to Calvary. There, he was nailed to the cross. People had gathered to watch. Some mocked Jesus as he was dying. Others mourned for him.

In Luke 23:34, Jesus said, "Father, forgive them, for they do not know what they are doing." And right before his final breath he spoke," IT IS FINISHED!" Jesus died and our sin was paid in full so we can have eternal life!

The WHIP, the HAMMER, and the CROSS. Three well-known instruments of agony. All important elements of a crucifixion. Jesus was murdered by the use of these items. They were the professional tools of death in the skillful hands of a Roman executioner! They slowly and painfully drained the life from Jesus our Lord and Savior with these items!

You didn't die immediately. No, that would have been too merciful. The WHIP, HAMMER & CROSS made sure that you died in slow-motion agony. The outcome was always certain to be death but the emphasis was on the maximum amount of pain and suffering!

I would like for us to focus on Jesus being flogged or whipped, His flesh was torn and by His strips we are healed.

Mark 15:15 "Pilate wanted to satisfy the crowd, so he released Barabas to them. He had Jesus flogged, and handed him over to be crucified."

The whip consisted of nine knotted thongs, with sheep bone and iron balls tied to the end to rip the flesh of anyone that was being flogged. They call this "the cat of nine tails".

The victim was stripped naked, strapped to a wooden post/pole, and flogged on his back, buttocks and legs by two Roman soldiers. The iron balls, sheep bones and leather thongs would cut deep into the skin, ripping tissue, tearing the underlying skeletal muscle and produced quivering ribbons of bleeding flesh. This is what they did to my Jesus that awful day in Jerusalem. I'm grieving in my spirit just thinking about this. The whip was the process in which we may be healed to receive the miracle!

The prophet Isaiah prophesied in Isaiah 53:5, *"He was wounded for our transgressions, he was bruised for our iniquities; the punishment that brought us peace was upon him, and by his stripes we are healed."*

Jesus paid the punishment of our sins! Every time the whip was swung and hit our Lord across his body, his flesh was removed, at that very moment prophesy from the Old Testament was being fulfilled.

Jesus gave up his physical flesh, that our flesh of the Spirit, our sin nature, may be forgiven, healed so that we can walk in freedom from the curse!

Jesus being whipped redeemed the curse of sickness. Jesus provided a way today for you and I to receive physical, mental and emotional healing!

Isaiah 53:5 states "and by his stripes we are healed."

Say this with me, "By His Stripes We Are Healed!" There is a miracle ready to take place.

Would you like to receive your healing?

The first step is acknowledging and meditating by faith that Jesus redeemed you!

Confess that you have been redeemed by Christ Jesus from the curse of sickness. Obtain God's Word and what it says that you can declare. Declaring and confessing God's Word will develop faith for healing. You must discover what the Word says about the promise of healing for you. Meditate day and night upon on scriptures of healing until your heart is settled on the fact that healing is God's will for you. There is a miracle waiting to happen in your life.

Proverbs 4:20-22 "My son, pay attention to what I say; turn your ear to my words. Do not let them out of your sight, keep them within your heart; for they are life to those who find them and health to one's whole body."

God's words are medicine for your physical, emotional, and spiritual health. The enemy, Satan, desires for you to operate in a mind of carnality, doubt and unbelief. In this state, miracles do not take place. He knows if he can get you to operate in these three areas you have defeated yourself, you are no longer meditating on God's Word and believing on the promises He has for you. God desires and wills us to function and operate in the supernatural.

James 1:6 says we are to "ask in faith, nothing wavering," or we will not receive what we desire from Him. Never give up! Stand strong! Do not let Satan lie to you or let others tell you your physical, emotional, and spiritual health cannot be changed. You serve a miracle-working God, and God wants to see you through. Your healing is a tool for sharing the testimony of what God has done in your life. Your miracle will give God glory and show the power of Christ Jesus. So ask in faith, not wavering, He is ready to manifest His healing power to you physically, emotionally and spiritually. Healing is coming your way in the Name of Jesus!

Continually confess and believe that "by Jesus' stripes, I was healed"—nothing wavering—and meditate on:

Isaiah 53:5 "But He was pierced for our transgressions, He was crushed for our iniquities; the punishment that brought us peace was on Him, and by His wounds we are healed."

1 Peter 2:24, "He himself bore our sins' in his body on the cross, so that we might die to sins and live for righteousness; 'by his wounds you have been healed'."

Matthew 8:17 "This was to fulfil what was spoken through the prophet Isaiah: 'He took up our infirmities and bore our diseases'."

Matthew 6:9-10 "This, then, is how you should pray: Our Father in heaven, hallowed be your name, your kingdom come, your will be done, on earth as it is in heaven."

It is God's will for you to be healed! Never accept the sickness, it does not belong to you. Your body is the temple of the Holy Spirit and is under attack. When your body is under attack, you must fight back in the Spirit. By proclaiming your healing in the Name of Jesus, and by meditating and confessing God's Word, you are operating the in Spirit.

1 John 5:14–15 "This is the confidence we have in approaching God: that if we ask anything according to His will, He hears us. And if we know that He hears us – whatever we ask – we know that we have what we asked of Him."

3 John 2 "Dear friend, I pray that you may enjoy good health and that all may go well with you, just as you are progressing spiritually."

Personal steps I have applied to my life is to ASK God, BELIEVE for miracle AND RECEIVE IN THE NAME OF JESUS. I want to encourage you to confess and meditate unto God and believe that you have received your healing right now!

Paul the Apostle wrote in Romans 8:32, "He who did not spare His own Son, but delivered Him up for us all, how shall He not with Him also freely give us all things?"

God gave His only Son Jesus Christ to pay the penalty of the curse of sin, diseases and death, so you can receive freely all things for the Glory of God! By the stripes of Jesus Christ may you receive your miracle in Jesus Name.

Pray this Prayer:

Father God, we thank You that Your Word says that Jesus took my infirmities and bore my sicknesses, and by whose stripes we were healed. Christ has redeemed us from every sickness, disease and pain. Lord, Your Word states in 3 John 2, that You wish above all things that we prosper and have good health. We thank You, God, for my healing and good health. It is so good to be redeemed from the curse of sickness!

According to Your inspired Word, every good gift and every perfect gift comes from You. Sickness, disease and pain are not perfect; therefore, they're not from You. Father, your son Jesus went around doing good and healing all that were oppressed of the devil, for you were with Him. According to the Word, healing is good and it comes from you. Sickness is not good; it comes from Satan.

Our body is a temple of the Holy Spirit, and Jesus gave us the authority to tread upon serpents and scorpions and over all the power of the enemy. Greater is He that is in us, than he that is in the world. The Name of Jesus is above every name. We refuse to allow any sickness, disease, pain or malfunction in our bodies, in the Name of Jesus.

Your healing has already been provided for you, receive your miracle!

CRAIG MCGEE serves as the Senior Pastor at Victory Life Church in Fayette County Tennessee. His passion is reaching people for the Gospel of Jesus Christ. Craig is married to Kristal and has three children CJ, Caleb, Kammy.

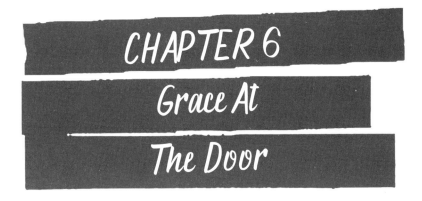

CHAPTER 6
Grace At
The Door

Pastor Chris Moore
ASHLAND CITY ASSEMBLY OF GOD

A twenty-three-year-old young man named Jim decided to go to church one Sunday. He had just finished college and had started applying for jobs. He had been to sixty different places and had been turned down at each because of the way he looked. There weren't too many employers looking for a guy like him; with long hair and a beard. He was looking for a place of hope but waiting to be rejected again. On that Sunday, as he neared the entrance to the church, he saw an older man. He thought, if anyone is going to reject me, it'll be him. He walked up to the man and looked him in the eyes, expecting him to turn away, ultimately rejecting him the way others had. He had made up his mind, if he rejects me, I'll never come to a church again. To his surprise, the man extended his hand and said, "Welcome brother, we're so glad you could be here with us today." In that moment, those words broke through all his defenses. Little did he know that this man, Brother Thurston, who was seventy-five years old, was one of the most spiritual and loving men in the church.

If you've been around church or Christians long enough, you've probably been hurt or know someone that's been hurt. Over and over I hear it, "Will Christians accept me? How are they going to act if I walk into church? Will they forgive me? I'm afraid everyone will be talking about me and judging me."

It shouldn't be that way, should it? As I've talked to people and studied those who have walked away from God and church, many times the number one concern isn't if God will forgive them. It's not even, does God still love me. The biggest concern is, will I be judged for the mistakes that I have made. Even as they ask for forgiveness from their Heavenly Father, they wonder if the church body, their brothers and sisters in Christ, will forgive them. And for some reason, they expect judgment and not love.

I don't believe Jesus wanted or intended for the church to be that kind of place where people fear being judged more than they expect to be loved. There's something wrong with that and with us, followers of Jesus, if that's the perception. There's something even more wrong if that's not perception but that's reality.

Unfortunately, this is not a new problem. In Jesus' day, there was a group of people called the Pharisees. They were a religious group and cultural leaders. They believed in strictly following the law, the Torah, completely. But following the written law wasn't enough. They then created a series of additional rules. They called these rules, the Oral Law. These additional laws were designed to help keep people from breaking the written law. They eventually wrote down these laws and it became more written law. These were not just the Ten Commandments. One of the books they were supposed to memorize and follow was over twelve thousand pages long. If you didn't follow all the laws, you were unworthy because you were breaking God's law.

When Jesus came, His message was completely different. His message challenged that thinking and those rules. Because of this, Jesus didn't get along very well with the Pharisees. They were all about the rules and Jesus shared and modeled something different, grace. This was the opposite message of the Pharisees. Jesus did some crazy things like love those who seemed unlovable. He crossed racial and ethnic lines. He was accepting of outsiders. He treated women and children with importance and significance. Jesus even healed people at the wrong time, the wrong places and in the wrong ways. Jesus said the wrong things. Jesus spent time with sinners and even ate with them. His actions went against everything the Pharisees believed and did. They had controlled the religious climate for many years. Their approach to God had influenced the culture and society.

There are always those that disagree, and I'm sure there were those in Jesus' day that disagreed with the Pharisees. If you were one that disagreed, you would be punished, rejected or even worse. So, either you lived up to the rules and followed them or you were judged publicly.

The Pharisees did the same thing that the body of Christ has been known to do. They were quick to judge, slow to forgive. Quick to criticize, slow to encourage. Maybe you know this crowd. The one that's quick to let everyone know what to do and how to do it. This was the very setting that surrounded Jesus. This is what made His message so significant to those who heard it.

In one of Jesus' most famous messages, the Sermon on the Mount, He points out a few things that are so important for us to know. This message is found in Matthew, chapter five to seven. As He began to unfold this wisdom and knowledge, the crowd was taken aback. This was a message they had longed to hear but never knew existed. As Jesus was sharing this message to the group of people, most likely in the crowd are Pharisees as well. In a culture and world of rules and regulations, Jesus said something earth shattering. He said, "Do not judge others, and you will not be judged. For you will be treated as you treat others. The standard you use in judging is the standard by which you will be judged" Matthew 7:1-2.

I've heard it said that the word 'judge' means when you make a pronouncement of someone else's spiritual condition based on your opinion. In other words, you decide the standard or measuring stick. You decide whether they are worth or unworthy. It's so easy to become judgmental. Many times, we become the judge and the jury. We decide in our hearts or even publicly if someone is guilty or not. But these two verses in Matthew should scare us to death. They should make us change our behavior. But all too often, we're harsh and unforgiving. Who wants to be judged by God this way? Let's be honest, if the way we judge others is the way we'll be judged, then we should want to show mercy and grace. Why? Because that's exactly what we'll want and need.

As Jesus is saying all of this, you can just imagine that the crowd begins to look at the chief judgers, the Pharisees. Of course, this would have made them mad. Then Jesus ask two questions like only He can. "And why worry about a speck in your friend's eye when you have a log in your own? How can you think of saying to your friend, 'Let me help you get rid of that speck in your eye,' when you can't see past the log in your own eye? Hypocrite! First get rid of the log in your own eye; then you will see well enough to deal with the speck in your friend's eye."

Something you never want to be called is a hypocrite. Why. Because a hypocrite is someone who pretends to live according to one set of rules and beliefs but doesn't. This is someone whose words sound good coming out of their mouth, but they just don't live it out.

I think everyone hates hypocrites. I think most of all, the hypocrite becomes disgusted with themselves and angry with those around them because they know they are living a lie. You see I was a hypocrite. I was surrounded by religion. I grew up in a home that honored God. I even had parents that loved Jesus. For many years I played the part and hid the truth. It's so easy in church or around Christians to fake it. To pretend you believe all the things you're agreeing with and even saying. But honestly, all being a hypocrite did for me was cheapen the truth because I didn't value it. I was using the truth of God for my own gain and agenda. After a while, it sickened me. Then I became someone that played the part but secretly was living another life. It's not hard to do. In fact, you can even get good at it. But what's the point of living like that? That's not living, that's existing. And I got tired of just existing one day. I got tired of the lies and weight of two separate lives. My world began to crash down around me. One night, at the age of seventeen, I was sitting on the floor in my room with all but one small light on. I was broken. And for the first time in many years tears began to run down my face. I was empty. Being a hypocrite had run its course. Now, what was I going to do?

Jesus said be honest with yourself. Don't be a hypocrite who pretends like you're perfect and flawless. Before you point out someone else's faults and failures, first deal with your own.

Jesus set a standard by which all Christ's followers should be judged. In John 13:34-35, Jesus said, "So now I am giving you a new commandment: Love each other. Just as I have loved you, you should love each other. Your love for one another will prove to the world that you are my disciples."

A hypocrite tries to act the part. But Jesus doesn't want actors, He wants disciples. People will know you're a disciple and follower of Jesus by how you treat others. Unfortunately, too often love and grace seem to get lost. Like Pharisees, we're often guilty of putting ourselves in the place of judge.

Before you tell someone else about their behavior, pray. I've seen some horrible situations where someone just had to set someone else straight. If you just have to do it, don't. You're probably not going to do it with the right spirit. If you have a problem with someone else's actions, take it to God and not other people. So often we do so much damage by gossiping. We call it many things like just sharing an opinion. Be very careful not to make yourself the judge. One thing that'll help keep us aligned to the Lord is regularly confessing our own sins to God. Getting real about yourself is a safeguard against becoming a hypocrite.

The message of grace shouldn't be cheap. It's not a do what you want and anything goes message. You see, one day we'll all stand before God, the ultimate judge. No one gets a free pass on this day. Be careful not to impose your personal style, preferences or convictions on others.

Instead, chose flexibility, understanding, forgiveness and grace.

Jim, the young man at the beginning of this chapter, was my dad. I often think if this man at the door would have rejected him and not shown grace, would I even be here and would I be serving the Lord? My dad went on to become very involved at that church. He met my mom at that place of worship. He eventually became the pastor at that church. Think of how my family tree could have changed if Brother Thurston hadn't shown the long-haired young man grace at the door.

I grew up in a pastor's home and around church. I thought I had it all together but then I came to a breaking point myself. Pretending is a lifeless place to be. I began the long journey of climbing out of the sewage of life I had gotten into. It didn't happen overnight and I ultimately had to remove myself from the very life I had created in order to get free and to truly know Him. The best thing a hypocrite, actor, or pretender can do is own up to who they really are and begin the journey of seeking an authentic, loving relationship with the Everlasting Father.

Love is when we overlook a multitude of shortcomings. Grace goes hand and hand with love.

To those who think they have it all together and find it easy to judge and not show grace, don't forget what Jesus took you out of and saved you from. We all need the grace and mercy of God.

To those who use grace to their own advantage and cheapen it, stop playing the game. There's so much more to Him. Let Jesus be the most influential person in your life.

*All scripture used is taken from the New Living Translation

CHRIS MOORE *serves as the Lead Pastor at Gateway Church Assembly of God in Ashland City, Tennessee. He and his wife Leslie have pastored Gateway since 2012. They are the proud parents of their daughter, Mia Moore.*

CHAPTER 7
Why the Church
Must Value People

Pastor Bobby Morgan
MEETING PLACE CHURCH

Roadkill. I didn't even know it was a real word. But roadkill was the word that immediately came to mind when I suddenly woke up about 3am contemplating how I would begin to write a chapter on grace and forgiveness. What's the correlation? Keep reading...

The official definition for "roadkill" woke me up even more than the coffee I'm sipping on as I write. The second part of the definition is the one that really hit at the core of what I want to say. The first part of the definition I could've written myself. I live in middle TN where everything from deer, possums, squirrels, groundhogs, skunks, and in recent days even the occasional armadillo are seen almost daily as carnage on the roads 'round here. So, the primary definition was as expected: "noun: roadkill - an animal (or animals, collectively) killed by a vehicle on a road." We all knew that, right? It was the second part, the "informal" definition that floored me: "someone (italics mine) or something no longer useful or desired." Then they added a phrase that someone might say if they were the unfortunate "someone" who felt no longer useful or desired: "Gee, thanks for making me feel like roadkill."

I don't remember the exact date. But, I do remember it was a hot, late summer day, probably around 1990. I was working for a linen company in Nashville, TN. One of the customers on my route was Nashville General Hospital. I serviced the morgue there with linens. Morgues are not the most pleasant places to have to frequent, especially when your job takes you into the very room where autopsies are being performed on the bodies of the recently, and sometimes not so recently, deceased. See, General Hospital is where the bodies of the unidentified, unclaimed and unrecognizable were sent to be, for lack of a better term, "disposed of properly". I saw some horrific sights while servicing linens there. But one day, one sight, one man sticks in my memory above all the others. This day, this sight, this man would change my view of people forever. I walked into the room adjacent to the forensics lab to get the linen order from the attendant and the smell when I opened the door to the hospital was indescribable. The attendant, much too calloused to the plight of the deceased, said to me with a chuckle: "Would you like to meet maggot man?" The ironic thing is I had just prayed before going in there: "Lord, I really don't want to see any dead people today." I felt I had seen enough. I'm the linen man, not the forensics expert or anything else in the medical, law or crime industry. I told the attendant "NO, I really don't want to meet maggot man." I even requested that he have someone bring the dirty linens out to me rather than me going in there and getting them myself. He, again chuckling, said, "No, you need to meet maggot man." So, determined to look away, I suited up in my hazmat gown and gloves and went in. I'll spare you the details, but what I saw laying on that cold, stainless steel table I don't believe even the modern horror film producers of our day could have reproduced, or even imagined if they tried. Friend, it's one thing to see a possum on the side of the road that's been there a few days in late August in Tennessee. But I assure you it is something altogether different to see a six foot, 200 lb man who was found in the woods of Percy Warner Park after laying there two or three weeks in the summer heat. The attendant told me that all indications were that he had committed suicide. Now, here's what forever changed my life and my ministry about that day: IMMEDIATELY when I saw the man I heard the Lord clearly say to me, "The thief does not come except to steal, and to kill, and to destroy.

I have come that they may have life, and that they may have it more abundantly" (John 10:10 NKJV). See, here was a MAN, a PERSON, made in the image of God! A MAN! Not roadkill! Not harvestable, or unharvestable organs! A PERSON! PURPOSEFUL! Fearfully and wonderfully made! ETERNAL! A man, who's name to this day I still don't know, but maybe that's because to me he's supposed to represent EVERYBODY!

The grace of God abounding from Calvary's Hill, that we sing about and preach about on Sundays, includes everything that would have turned this man's life around and dispelled the darkness and the lies of the enemy that had him believing that all was lost and hopeless. Mankind, in our fallen state, is duped and susceptible to the consequence of sin and the lies of the enemy. But, God the Father, in spite of the fact that we fell and sinned against Him, values the relationship with man so much that He sent Jesus to die to restore our relationship with Him. He places so much VALUE on us that He literally sent His Son to die to restore the relationship with us, both now and for eternity. And there is no one any more valuable to Him than anyone else. Everyone conceived is precious and valuable and eternal; and it's His desire that we spend eternity with Him. That's pretty standard preaching, but we need to grasp the truth in our dark day that God paid the same price for EVERYONE and it was the highest price that could be paid. Therefore, He proved that all men and women, boys and girls are precious and valuable to Him. And the purpose of this writing is to say that we, as God's people, must value people as well if we're ever going to have the sense of urgency, the compassion and the love needed to do whatever it takes to reach the lost and hurting with the Gospel.

I love acrostics. I think they are a great and memorable way to teach. Here is an acrostic that came out of my fateful encounter at General Hospital that day.

The church must value people because **P.E.O.P.L.E** are:
Precious to God:
"You made all the delicate, inner parts of my body and knit me together in my mother's womb. Thank you for making me so

*wonderfully complex! Your workmanship is marvelous— how well
I know it. You watched me as I was being formed in utter seclusion,
as I was woven together in the dark of the womb. You saw me before
I was born. Every day of my life was recorded in your book. Every
moment was laid out before a single day had passed. How precious
are your thoughts about me, O God" Psalm 139:13-17.*

Now, I could remind you that the person who gets on your last
nerve, God made that person, loves that person, meticulously formed
that person in their mother's womb, and has a plan for everyday of
their life, etc… But, I think part of the breakdown in our valuing that
person the way God does lies in the fact that we didn't MAKE that
person. We don't think about that person all the time. We didn't write
a book with all that person's tomorrows in it. The fact is, we don't have
the vested interest in people that God does. There's no way we could
pay the price He did for people. But, here's the kicker! He also sees
the people around you as so precious, that He empowered YOU to be
a witness to them. He put healing in your hands for them and wants
to use you to show them the love of Jesus. Because every person is
precious to God.

Expendable in today's society: Matt. 24:12 – "And because iniquity
shall abound, the love of many shall wax cold." 2 Tim 3:3 says that one
of the characteristics of people in the last days will be "UNLOVING".
The KJV "without natural affection." I could go on and on with the
senseless murders and acts of violence and abortion in our world
today, but you watch the news like I do. What I'm really trying to get
us to see is that while the world is growing colder and colder, and more
and more apathetic and numb to people, God is working within the
church to be conformed more and more into the image of His Son!
That means as they get darker, we get brighter. As they grow colder,
we get warmer. As they get less loving, we get more loving. Jude 21-22
says for us to keep ourselves in the love of God and show mercy to
people and snatch them from the fire.

On purpose: Jesus said in John 12:32 "If I be lifted up I will draw
ALL MEN unto Me." If Jesus is drawing on all men to be saved, then

God has a purpose and a plan for everybody. We need to be letting people know that there's more to life than living for a paycheck. There's more to life than trying to cram your life full of things that don't satisfy. People need something to live for! And they're never gonna be fulfilled till they're doing what God created them for and that's to worship and have a relationship with Him.

Pliable: They can be bent and shaped. Prov. 22:6 says "Train up a child in the way they should go and when they are old they'll not depart from it." That means children can be shaped toward their destiny in God. Now, I don't have to tell you that the Devil has an agenda to see that children are not getting trained up in the way that they should go. The banning of prayer and Bible reading in our public class rooms that happened in 1962 has now progressed into a blatant teaching of everything ungodly and people are pliable. And the church, specifically Christian parents, have to be adamant to get the Word of God into our children! And churches have to preach the truth without compromise.

Liable: It means they are accountable and responsible. Heb. 9:27 "As it is appointed unto man once to die but after this the judgment." The church must value people because every person is going stand before God. And 2 Cor. 5:20-21 tells us that we are CHRIST'S AMBASSADORS who are to be imploring people to be reconciled to God through Christ. In Luke 14:23 Jesus said "Go out into the highways and hedges and COMPEL them to come in." "COMPEL" is a strong word. It means you stay after them in love. You don't let up! Why? Because people are…

Eternal: Never forget that every person you see, regardless of where you see them - if you go to a football game and there are 65,112 people there - that's 65,112 people who are going to spend ETERNITY in one of two places. Matt. 25:46 – Jesus says in that day when all men stand before God, there'll only be two groups of people. One group will go away into ETERNAL punishment, and the righteous to ETERNAL life. And God extended His grace and forgiveness through Jesus so that none would perish.

Not long ago one of our little girls in church came up to me and handed me a gold chocolate coin. She said this when she gave it to me: "It's the only one I have and I want you to have it." Of course I said "thank you." Then she said again, "It was my only one, but I'm giving it to you." God looked at humanity and gave His ONLY Son. That's how much He values people. He wants us to value people enough to tell them about His gift.

BOBBY MORGAN serves as the Senior Pastor at Meeting Place Church in Fairview, Tennessee. Bobby has been married to his wife Darlene of this writing, nearly 35 years, and he has 3 children, Daniel, Ryan and Sydne and 8 wonderful grandchildren.

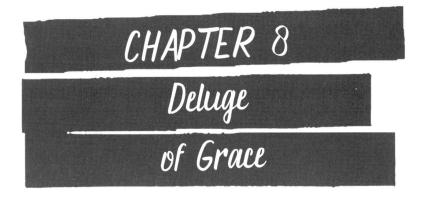

CHAPTER 8
Deluge
of Grace

Pastor David Morgan
UNITED CHURCH LAWRENCEBURG

For the grace of God has appeared that offers salvation to all people. It teaches us to say "No" to ungodliness and worldly passions, and to live self-controlled, upright and godly lives in this present age (Titus 2:11-12).

Fogged up windows and the roar of a 289 two barrel V-8 in that old 1967 Ford Mustang was the usual scene for my friends and me on cold January nights in southern middle Tennessee. It was just another night driving backroads with my closest friends doing what we liked to do; getting high, drinking and blasting music from the 6x9's in the rear deck, artists ranging from Led Zeppelin to TuPac Shakur. We were just four teenagers trying to figure things out. Little did we know there was much more to life than what we had experienced. That old tape deck in my Stang had always proven faithful and cassette tapes were half the cost of CD's, so I had plenty to go around. Teenage life, in small town USA, left you with few recreational options in the mid 90's - cruising backroads and getting messed up just seemed the thing to do. It soon became obvious that there was much more on the agenda this night than any of us could have imagined.

Growing up as the 5th son to an Assemblies of God minister, I was afforded the privilege of having several role models whether I wanted them or not. I use the word "privilege" today, but that was not how I looked at it back then. I can honestly say, that my home life was not legalistic and controlling; it was loving and edifying, but for some reason I chose to follow a different path. My friends' opinions and the music and party culture of the 90's seemed to appeal to me more than the "religiosity" that had helped establish a stable childhood and home life. I took for granted the blessings of God on my family and began to doubt His very existence. That cold January night I was as far from God as I had ever been and there was nothing I could do about it.

Cruising at a controlled and focused speed of about 20 MPH, as was the norm for most pot-heads, the car became filled with smoke and things started to get going. Everything became hilarious. We were getting to that place we had been anticipating all day at school; after all, it was Friday! As things began to ratchet up, one of my friends leaned up from the backseat and whispered, "Hell's Bells." I knew exactly what he wanted, a change in the mood. Reaching under the driver's seat I pulled out the cassette tape case and scrolled through to AC-DC's "Back in Black" album. I flipped it to side-one, track one, inserted it into the dashboard tape player and pressed play. The anticipation was wrecking me and my senses were heightened by the drugs we had just inhaled. I was ready, not to just listen to the song, but to feel it—a song about hell, Satan, and his plan of destruction for me. Seemed harmless, right? After all, it was just musical entertainment - just rock-n-roll. Music might have seemed to be innocent, but I learned that night that things are not always as they seem.

Reaching for the volume knob, I cranked it to the threshold of distortion. We were ready. The guys asked, "What did you put in?" "Just wait, you'll know it from the first note," I replied. But nothing ever happened. I pressed rewind and hit play again, no sound, no music, nothing! Ejecting the tape I took a closer look to see if it was damaged, but it looked fine. By this time the guys were dying to know what song I had selected but I still remained silent. I fast forwarded to track 2 "Shoot to Thrill," and it played. I did the same for track 3, 4 and 5 – they all played! Frustrated, I ejected the tape, flipped it to the other side and pressed play. Every track on that side played as well. At this point I was getting angry. I stopped the car, cursed the tape player (as if that would work), blew in the tape (that always worked), put it back in, rewound to track one, side one, pressed play…. Nothing! At this point I was using every word I had NEVER heard my dad say. I was literally freaking out – screaming out, "I just want Hell's Bells!"

Then, BAM! There it was. Like a snowball to the face! The clearest, most loving, and sincere voice I had ever heard.

As my friends looked on and wondered what was going on with me, I was in another world! I had this unreal, unprecedented and transcendent spiritual moment. Looking back on it now, it's like everything was paused and it was just me and Jesus in the car. He spoke to me in the most gentle voice and said, "Son, I won't let it play, so please stop trying!" At this point in my life I had never heard the voice of God so clearly. I had never felt His love in such a real and tangible way. It was as if nothing else mattered to Him in that moment than getting through to me. It was there, in that red 1967 Mustang, on a cold January night with the same old friends doing the same old things, angry and full of worldliness, that I had a personal encounter with God's unmerited favor – **GRACE!**

Perplexed and astonished that He would go to such lengths to speak to me, I sobered up almost immediately. As the guys looked on with stunned faces, I slowly reached for the chrome window handle and began to gently turn it until it was all the way down. No one said a word. I then reached for the tape deck and hit eject, grabbed the tape, and threw it out the window as far as I could. Still, not talking, the guys watched in silence. I reached for the handle again and started cranking the window back up until it was closed. Still, not a word from the others. I put the 'Stang in gear, pressed the accelerator, eased off the clutch, and on we went. At this point, all of us just looked ahead trying to make sense of what had just happened. I turned my head to the right and my buddy just looked at me and gave the "man nod," somehow I believe he knew what was going on. He was the only one in the car, other than myself, that had a spiritual upbringing. There was no need to exchange words in that moment. We both simply turned our gazes forward and let it be.

Previously, I referred to this moment as the first time I had encountered God's grace. And that's exactly what it was. I discovered that day that God's grace is free - free of charge, free of blame, free of pretense, and freely given. What blew me away in that moment was that, in spite of my sinfulness and obvious destructive mindset, He broke through to speak to me anyway! That's Grace! God breaking through the darkness; not because He has to, but rather because He wants to. I had my first personal taste of His grace that day and I liked it. It was more real to me than the drugs I used. More real in that moment than anything I had ever experienced. Of course, God's grace was already at work in my life, through my family my upbringing and provision. But this was the first time He'd ever broken through just to speak to me, about me. He taught me that day that His grace is personal, customized and packaged individually for everyone.

Personal Grace

It would be great to say that I fell to my knees that night, repented of my sin, and got right with God. But unfortunately, I did not. I was more stubborn than that! That cold January night was just the beginning, the first drop in God's bucket of Love and Grace in my life. It was no longer my parent's religion; it was mine. For the first time in my life there was now another cup in my heart other than the one I had grown accustomed to drinking from. Drop by drop, day by day, God began to fill up this cup, this bucket; and it was good. By His grace, God deposited in me over the next few years what would soon tip the balance in my life. I would soon find myself no longer simply sprinkled by occasional encounters with His grace, but I'd be engulfed by it - a deluge of His unconditional and unmerited favor flooding me. Over the next eighteen months, I wandered deeper and deeper into sin and the darkness that accompanies it. Yet, Jesus, continued to pour out His love for me in unprecedented ways. These encounters went from what once seemed distant and merely religious to becoming the most personal and real relationship I had ever known! I finally got it! He loves me – it was now more than just a cliché - it was real! I was being washed and cleansed by His grace, not because I deserved it, but because He truly cares about what's best for me. I had a taste of the living water Jesus offered the woman at the well in John 4:10, "If you knew the gift of God, and who it is that asks you for a drink, you would have asked him and he would have given you living water….. whoever drinks this water will never thirst again."

This water, by which I had now been engulfed, was changing me. I began to hunger and thirst for what was real and eternal instead of what was fake and temporal. The blinders were off and my heart was free! October 15, 1997 I accepted His love for me. By His **GRACE** I was saved. I did not deserve it, nor did I earn it, His grace is free!

The Power of Grace

I celebrated twenty years free from the curse and bondage of sin on October 15, 2017. The past twenty years have been incredible. God has done things in my life with regularity that are undeniably His doing and working. I'm amazed, overwhelmed, and flooded by His loving grace on a daily basis. It is still astonishing to me that as big as God is, He will "Stop a tape from playing," just to let me know that He cares! I have learned the hard way in my walk with the Lord that I cannot earn His favor; it is His, and His alone to give. Grace, simply defined is: unmerited and undeserved favor, approval, acceptance, or esteem. **God holds us in high esteem, not because we are perfect, but rather, because we are His.** This has never been articulated better than in Paul's letter to the church in Ephesus.

"For it is by grace you have been saved, through faith – and this is not from yourselves, it is the gift of God – not by works, so that no one can boast" (Ephesians 2:8-9 NIV).

So, what comes first: Grace... or Faith? For me, the answer to that question came on an old country backroad where I was as far from faith as I had ever been. God's grace flooded my life, stopped time, and changed something in the physical realm, all to give me a glimpse into what was eternal. I encountered His grace that day and I have learned to trust and depend on it ever since. There is **POWER** in His Grace! As Titus 2:11-12 states, "His Grace teaches us to say NO to ungodliness and worldly passions, and to live self-controlled, upright and godly lives in this present age . . . In my weakness, the strength of His grace is made known. **Let the Deluge of Grace** flood your life.

"Trust in the Lord, lean not on your own understanding, acknowledge Him in all your ways, and He will direct your paths" *(Proverbs 3:5).*

DAVID MORGAN *serves as the Lead Pastor of United Church in Lawrenceburg, Tennessee. He and his wife Stephanie have five children and all serve together in changing their region with the love of Christ.*

CHAPTER 9
Finding Forgiveness
in Style

Pastor Jason Murphy
COLLIERVILLE ASSEMBLY OF GOD

I had not been preaching that long when I received an invitation to conduct revival services for a church on the bayou in Louisiana. I was living in Nashville, TN at the time and was serving as a Youth Pastor in an Assembly of God church. My wife and I are from Louisiana. So needless to say, I eagerly accepted the invitation and looked forward to preaching in my home state.

The date of the revival finally arrived. We loaded up the car and headed south. We arrived to our destination late on a Saturday night. The next morning, we woke up eager to minister. If I remember correctly, not much happened that morning. However, that night the church was filled and excitement was in the air. The service was powerful. Everything seemed to be anointed by the Lord, including the guy giving the announcements and the ushers who received the offering! The expectancy was electric in the atmosphere. As the altar time was winding down, I was approached by a young man. He said, "I am a stylist and I can't help but noticing that you need a haircut. I am normally not open on Monday's, but if you would like I will open up just for you and give you a haircut." It was true. I did need a haircut! My schedule had been crazy and I simply did not make the time to get a haircut before leaving to minister in this church. So, I agreed and we settled on a time.

Monday dawned. I arrived at the shop and knocked on the door. The young man opened the door, greeted me, and invited me in. When I walked into the shop, I noticed that the lights were dim, instrumental music was playing, and incense was burning. I thought to myself, "This is a little odd, but he said he was a stylist and not a barber, so I guess I will go with it." I was directed to the chair where he washed hair. After he washed my hair, I was directed to the styling chair. I sat down. He covered me with the apron, grabbed his instruments, and went to work. As he worked, we talked. He brought up a few points from my sermon that I preached the night before. Then he said something to the effect, "I listened to what you were saying last night about God giving us the power and the ability to overcome sin when He saves us. I have been going to church for a while now, but I am struggling to overcome the sin in my life." Out of nowhere I said something like, "You battle sexual sin not because God has not empowered you to overcome it, but because you refuse to forgive the one who hurt you." He stopped cutting my hair and spun the chair around so that we were looking face to face as opposed to the reflection from the mirror. He said, "What did you say?" I thought, "Great. He is offended, or I did not hear from God correctly. Either way, I am leaving here with half a haircut." I said, "I do not mean to be offensive or to hurt you in any way, but the Holy Spirit revealed to me that you are dealing with sexual perversion because you refuse to forgive someone." He said, "My dad abused me my whole life, and not just me, but my brother too. Why should I forgive him?" I said, "You should forgive him because no one is worth going to Hell over. Furthermore, you should forgive him because in reality your sin was just as offensive to God as your dad's sin is to you yet God forgave you and saved you." Tears welled up in his eyes. He asked, "Can you stay for a while? I am going to call my brother and ask him to come up here. He needs to hear this too." I said, "Sure."

A few minutes later, there was a knock on the door. The stylist opens the door and greets his brother. He walked him over to where I was sitting and said, "You have to listen to this guy. He is a preacher. He is here from Nashville to hold a revival at that church on the bayou. He told me that we needed to forgive dad." He looked at me and said something to the effect, "He abused us in horrible ways. Due to that abuse my brother has battles and I battle anger and rage and addictions, and you walk in here and say, 'You need to forgive him.' Who do you think you are?" I said a quick prayer under my breath, and then said, "I am no one. I am only a minister of the Gospel. I will tell you what I told your brother. You need to forgive him because no one is worth going to Hell over. Secondly, you need to forgive him because in reality your sin was just as offensive to God as your dad's sin is to you, yet God forgave you and saved you." The two brothers stood there and listened as I preached the Gospel, and talked about forgiveness. By the end of the conversation, they both vowed to forgive their dad, and they prayed to strengthen their commitment to serving Christ. I do not know what happened to the brothers or if they stayed faithful to Christ. I may not remember all the details of that day so many years ago, but I never forgot the lessons that I learned when the Lord used that encounter to teach me a few things about forgiveness and grace.

The *first* thing I learned is that we must never take for granted that someone has heard the Gospel. The brothers were attending church and had listened to hundreds of sermons. No doubt a few of those sermons dealt with the basics of the Gospel as well as the basics of forgiveness. However, just because someone listens to a message does not necessarily mean that they heard the message. Furthermore, God has a divine time in which He opens people's ears, minds and hearts to receive the message. We are not in control of the timing in which someone hears the Message. We are only responsible to present the Message. Never tire of presenting the Gospel. "It is the power of God unto salvation", and you never know when God is opening up a human heart to receive the greatest message in the world, the Gospel.

The *second* thing I learned was the greatness of God's grace. Earlier I mentioned that the brothers needed to forgive their dad because God forgave them. When one truly understands what Christ did on the Cross, then he truly gets a glimpse of how great God's grace is. Romans 5:8 reads, "But God commendeth his love toward us, in that, while we were yet sinners, Christ died for us."

Ephesians 1:3-7 reads

"Blessed be the God and Father of our Lord Jesus Christ, who hath blessed us with all spiritual blessings in heavenly places in Christ: According as he hath chosen us in him before the foundation of the world, that we should be holy and without blame before him in love: Having predestinated us unto the adoption of children by Jesus Christ to himself, according to the good pleasure of his will, To the praise of the glory of his grace, wherein he hath made us accepted in the beloved. In whom we have redemption through his blood, the forgiveness of sins, according to the riches of his grace."

From these we learn that God so loved His children that He planned to forgive us and save us by sending His Son, Jesus, to die on the Cross for our sins in order to wipe out, or cancel, the sin debt that we owed God. He planned to do all this, including saving you, even before creation! Furthermore, the Word teaches that He was raised to life again in order to justify us or to make us righteous in His sight. The amazing thing is that God did all this while we were yet sinners! He extended grace to us when we did not deserve it. He loved us, made a way to forgive us through the birth, death and resurrection of His Son; and then called us to Himself so that we might be forgiven, saved, healed, and delivered. He did all these things while we were sinners and did not deserve His grace, His mercy, or His forgiveness, but He gave it to us anyway! That is the greatness of God's grace. When we understand that we have been saved by God's great grace and that He has forgiven us of our sin and offense to Him, it is easy and natural to forgive those who have sinned against us and who have offended us.

The third thing I learned in this encounter is the power of unforgiveness. 2 Corinthians 2:10-11 reads, "To whom ye forgive any thing, I forgive also: for if I forgave any thing, to whom I forgave it, for your sakes forgave I it in the person of Christ; Lest Satan should get an advantage of us: for we are not ignorant of his devices."

The key is "lest Satan should take advantage of us; for we are not ignorant of his devices." Paul reminds us that we need to forgive people or Satan will use our unforgiveness as a device against us. Often times the device manifests as division in the home, church and relationships; it causes separation between people and God. Unforgiveness causes one not to truly and fully experience God's forgiveness. Matthew 6:14-15 reads, "For if ye forgive men their trespasses, your heavenly Father will also forgive you: But if ye forgive not men their trespasses, neither will your Father forgive your trespasses." We must truly forgive those who have sinned against us. If we do not forgive others, God will not forgive us our sins. Our inability to forgive others is a sign that we have not truly experienced God's forgiveness. If we have truly received and experienced God's forgiveness, then it is natural to forgive those who sinned against us because we realize just how much we have been forgiven of. That is why I stated that no one is worth going to Hell over. Sin is sin no matter how it manifests. Your sin against God is not less than those who have sinned against you. In fact, it is greater! If God has forgiven you of your sin, then you can forgive those who have sinned against you.

I plead with you; forgive those who have sinned against you so that you can move forward in life. If you will forgive, no matter how difficult it may be, you will experience God's grace, find freedom, and live out God's best for your life. He has great things in store for you!

Oh yeah. The stylist finished giving me a haircut. It was the best haircut that I have ever had! Talk about finding forgiveness in style!

JASON MURPHY is the Lead Pastor of Collierville First Assembly in Collierville, TN. He is known for his love and knowledge of theology, history, and political theory which is evident in his preaching/teaching ministry.

CHAPTER 10
Grace & Forgiveness
A Father' Dream Time

Pastor Nate Newell
TURNING POINT CHURCH

Love wins. I'm not sure who originally coined the phrase, but I heard it from my pastor for years. Over and over he would repeat it. Honestly, it took that repetition for it to take root in my heart. It's hard to have truly learned something until there comes a moment, or moments, when it is put to the test; when there is an opportunity for it to be applied. It just so happens that grace and forgiveness fall into that category of tests that every single one of us will face on multiple occasions.

My father was a wonderful man. He was a man who loved God and loved his family. A faithful provider, a wise counselor, kind and compassionate, and an incredible example of a servant leader. The strong and silent type to be sure; he didn't always say much, but when he did, everyone listened. Dad would normally leave the cooking to mom, which was definitely the right decision, because she was phenomenal at it. But every once in a while, he would make a couple of his specialties like scrambled eggs or perfectly grilled steaks. My father was the most generous man I've ever known. He was the father many dream of having. He was Superman.

There were so many uncharted emotions following the loss of my father. You find out real fast that the grief process isn't over in a month or two. The slightest memory, the smell of something cooking, a stretch of familiar road, anything can trigger the emotions connected with the loss of someone you love. It comes in waves; cycles of sadness. And deep loss leaves you completely exposed and vulnerable. Your emotions are on edge and your ability to appropriately interpret what is going on around you is skewed.

Having been unfamiliar with loss on this level, there was much I was ignorant about. And one of the critical and most difficult discoveries was that each family member processed grief differently. I assumed everyone would walk through grief the same way (that's code for thinking everyone would walk through it the same way I did). Family relationships feel a heavy strain when everyone is trying to handle it their own way. One family member can't stop crying, while another shuts down and shuts everyone out. One wants to pretend like nothing happened, while another feels like there's nothing worth living for. It's hard. And there's no avoiding it in this life. At some point we all experience the reality of losing someone we love very much. It's only by His grace that we can traverse those stormy waters and come to a place of peace and rest in Him.

It was during this process of grieving for my father that grace for each other was definitely put to the test. Why is it that living in a heart of grace and forgiveness is sometimes hardest with those closest to us? Our feelings of hurt, pain, and betrayal don't come from mere acquaintances or superficial relationships. The deepest wounds come from the closest relationships. The fact that a relationship is strong and deep is what qualifies it to experience the pains and struggles.

Often our familiarity can produce unhealthy assumptions about how another is feeling and we can start reacting based on those assumptions instead of the truth. Before you know it, there is hurt on top of hurt. Grace and forgiveness has to transition from being something that God gives to us, to being what we give to each other.

When someone hurts you, the knee jerk reaction is that you want them to hurt too. If you're suffering, you want them to suffer. Something in you wants them to know what it feels like to bleed like you're bleeding. And for some reason we tend to think that this is the only way to resolve our own hurt. But that's not the truth. Like Paul said to the Corinthians, "still there is a better way." That better way is love the love that paves the way for grace and forgiveness to flow. The truth is personified through Jesus. If Jesus had left love in the garden, He would have never made it to the cross.

Forgiveness is grace in action. Forgiveness is the evidence that grace is at work. Some of Jesus' most powerful words came from the most painful moments on the cross. At the time of unspeakable turmoil and pain, hurt and betrayal, Jesus reached into the depths of His soul for the words shattered time and space; the words that will heal our history and free our future - "Father forgive them, they don't know what they do." Indescribable grace! Unfathomable forgiveness! Unapologetic love! His forgiveness for us was and is grace in its fullest measure.

There is no Plan B with God. If we think that the cross, that the sacrifice of Jesus, was just God's reaction to the fall of man, we're missing one of the most important truths about the God we serve. His perfect will is just that, perfect. He knows the end from the beginning. And God had a plan of grace to forgive us and redeem us since the beginning. Jesus was the plan of grace and forgiveness all along. He was the Lamb who was slain *before* the foundations of the world. Before God created Adam and Eve, Jesus was the plan. Before God visited Abraham, Jesus was the plan. Before Moses delivered a nation, before David was crowned king, before the prophets spoke of what was to come, Jesus was the plan. And what better picture of grace is there of a God who, knowing the measure of grace and love that would be required of Him and His Son, would still choose to say, "let us make man in our own image?" It's the same grace He poured out when he created you and I. Remember what He said to Jeremiah? "Before I formed you in the womb, I knew you." Knowing we would fall, knowing we would fail, knowing we would miss the mark, make sinful and immoral choices, He still came to the most astounding conclusion - it's worth it! We are worth it to Him! How does Jesus choose disciples that would question Him, frustrate Him, try to rebuke Him, abandon Him and even betray Him? Grace. Sometimes it's hard to receive that kind of grace because we truly cannot comprehend how vast it is. But that's the kind of gifts God give - the best ones.

God is an incomparable gift giver. He's obsessed with giving. He gives new mercies every morning, unparalleled wisdom for anyone who asks, beauty for ashes, gladness for mourning, peace for hopelessness. God's got the giving thing down. He's the most generous being ever known. And that overwhelming generosity is propelled from His perfect love. "For God so *loved* the world He *gave*." When God makes a decision to give, He gives the absolute best. He saw us in our sinful and broken condition and sent the gift of His Son. And if you, being evil fathers, know how to give good gifts to your children, how much more will your Heavenly Father give good gifts to His children? Gifts like grace.

Grace is one of His most benevolent gifts. He is not stingy with His grace or His forgiveness. He abundantly pardons. His grace is sufficient; it is more than enough. That means it's equal to the task, it's up to the challenge. His grace can handle it. And even more than that, where sin increased, grace increased all the more. What a wonderful picture of a God who can't be defeated in any way! Not even His grace can lose! Grace has a perfect record.

Technically, for a gift to be a gift it must be received. God's grace and forgiveness was never meant to stop when it got to you or me. He expected then for us to take that gift and give it to someone else. The evidence that God's grace is at work in our lives is not necessarily in how much we receive but in how much we give. If we have freely received, then the heart of God within us should compel us to freely give.

Jesus tells a parable in Luke 7 where a moneylender had two debtors: one who owed five hundred days' wages and one who owed fifty days. They were both unable to repay and the moneylender graciously forgave them both. He then followed this short illustration with a question to Simon the Pharisee whose house he was visiting. "Which of the debtors will love the moneylender more?" Simon answered, "I suppose the one whom he forgave more." And Jesus responded to him, "You have judged correctly." Jesus uses what is happening in that moment to reveal the truth of His story and ends by sharing that the one who has been forgiven much loves much. But the one who has been forgiven little, loves little.

This parable is not only about the amounts the debtors owed. It's not really about who has more sin or less sin. We're all in the same boat. "All have sinned and fall short of the glory of God." This account is about the one who comes to a place of awareness and honesty with themselves. It's about what happens when that forgiveness is received.

What we are willing to give is evidence of what we have received. When Peter was entering through the Beautiful Gate and a man begging for alms called out to him, Peter's response was not what the man was expecting. He didn't have the silver and gold to meet the need and therefore could not give it. But what he did have, he was able and willing to give. He had received the name, the power, the faith, the man Jesus Christ, and gave Him away as freely as He had received Him. The wondrous miracle that resulted was because Peter gave what he had. We can't give something we don't have.

Grace and forgiveness serve as the formula, the recipe for restoration. Restoration is a high priority with the Father. God gave us grace not just because that's who He is or what He does, but also because we desperately needed it. It is a gift we haven't earned and we certainly don't deserve. He also knew that we would experience many moments in our lives where we would need to give that same grace to someone else. He knew that if we would give the same forgiveness He gave us, we would find freedom for our brother, our friend, and for ourselves. Grace and forgiveness are the Dream Team of Unity.

They work together to bring restoration between husbands and wives, parents and children, brothers and sisters. How do we know it will work? This is the recipe He used to restore the divided relationship between Himself and His children. And it is that same recipe that is the key to the restoration of every relationship.

Because God freely gave me His daily grace while grieving the loss of my father, I needed to give that same grace to my family members who were grieving in ways different from myself. In giving this grace, it released myself and my loved ones to grieve in our own ways. Forgiveness helped restore those family relationships that had become strained under the weight of grief. Ultimately, giving grace and forgiveness is one of the best and most healing ways we can show the love of our Heavenly Father.

In the end, every one of God's gifts flows from love. And love always wins. Love wins a brother. Love wins a son. Love wins the lost. Love wins the neglected, the hurting, the forgotten. If we are to ever express the Father's Dream Team of Forgiveness and grace in our lives, it can only come from the heart of love.

NATHAN NEWELL serves as the Lead Pastor of Turning Point Church in Murfreesboro, TN. He and his wife Ivy have been married twelve years and have four boys.

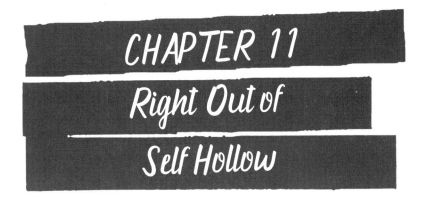

CHAPTER 11
Right Out of
Self Hollow

Pastor Chris Reneau
THE MEADOW CHURCH

When you consider grace and forgiveness, you must take into account the context of which a person is born and reared. The environment that we are raised in has an impact on our lives. Some influences of our upbringing are positive and some are negative. The first few years of a child's life are very important in their development. These are the formative years.

My life was largely influenced by a very dysfunctional family. My dad came from a larger family in Newport, TN. He had eleven brothers and sisters. For Dad, growing up in the East Tennessee mountains had its advantages and challenges. He lived a simple, carefree life, but was extremely poor. My dad's life as he grew up was characterized by working hard as a sharecropper's son. He missed a lot of school, drank, fought, and caroused. Both of his parents were Godly people. Dad recalled numerous occasions when his father and mother went to church, reading the Bible, and of the sounds of prayer filling their tiny country home. My mother, on the other hand, was raised in Rockford, TN, on Self Hollow Road in a middle-class home, by a down-to-earth, hard- working father and a loving, nurturing mother. Dad and Mom's lives were almost opposite when it came to socioeconomics. My dad's family moved from Newport to Self Hollow Road where he and Mom met, began dating, and soon married at a young age. Daddy continued his sinful lifestyle into their marriage. The chains of multiple bondages gripped his mortal soul. Both of my parents had God fearing and church going influences; although, it did not seem to take root in them!

They began to bring children into the world in the midst of marital strife and conflict. I was born the second of five kids. We moved to Maryville, TN to begin our lives trying not to depend on my mother's parents. My earliest memories of being raised were a mixed bag. On one hand, we were a close-knit family. On the other hand, turmoil filled our lives due to poverty, sin dominating our lives, and the absence of conviction to serve the Lord. Folks have asked me through the years, how did you know you were poor as a kid? Well, we lived in small houses, usually with no electricity, at times with no running water, and with very little food. We always were needing a vehicle due to them being broken down or our inability to pay for them. With one financial struggle after another, we moved back to Self Hollow Road in Rockford, TN, to be close to both Dad's and Mom's parents, as well as aunts and uncles. I remember family reunions, big gatherings, Sunday dinners, and a host of other sweet memories. But Dad was an outcast due to his inability to provide for us. We were always looked down upon.

One house I remember was an old coal house. The only source of heat was a coal heater. It was a four-room house that was either too hot or too cold and had no indoor plumbing. I would live on the same road until I turned 20 years old. In this same area, I would start riding the school bus as a kindergartner and I would ride it every day until I graduated high school. Daddy would work hard, and Momma would keep house. At times, Mom would find a waitressing job to help make ends meet. At 7 to 8 years old, smoking, chewing tobacco, cursing, drinking, fighting, and numerous other things were highly encouraged and accepted in our family.

Church and God for us were reserved for occasional special events like Easter, Christmas, or Homecoming services. There was a consciousness of God in my life, but no conviction. I was shy and introverted around crowds. I can tell you that I thought about a better life, but I didn't know how to get there. I can't forget the cold mornings with little or no heat in our small home, baths in the same water my entire family had used. I also cannot forget the cold walks to the school bus with a wet head because of no electricity, and of course no blow dryer to dry my hair. My hair would literally freeze, thaw, and drip after stepping onto a bus with heat. Free breakfast and free lunch were arranged for us at school due to our poverty. It was humiliating to be so young and having to audibly voice "free lunch" to the school cafeteria cashier as we went through the food lines. This course would stay the same all the way until I graduated high school.

Those early years and contextual moments in my life shaped me to who I would become. I wanted to excel at something. I was born with athletic ability. I was fast, agile, and driven by an inner toughness and a strong-will fashioned by my circumstances. I played all kinds of sports and was very good at most of them. In many of these sports, I was featured in the newspapers, magazines, won trophies and district and state awards. Although I was shy, I began to grow in popularity. I covered my shyness by being the class clown! I was soon hanging out with the "in-kids." The fail-safe for me when things were not going well was to turn to the negative behavioral patterns that my father had modeled all my life. At ages 12 to 13, I was already drinking moon shine, smoking, and always dipping or chewing tobacco. I smoked my first marijuana joint when I was in 8th grade. It was passed around in a car I was riding in with some guys, and I got "high." That day planted a seed of an addictive desire that snared me!

My home life soon got worse! False hopes and dreams, fussing, and fighting between Mom and Dad in open display in our little house trailer created a living hell for us. I have since realized that I can't blame my parents for the addictions I had, but all the stuff that we endured contributed to my bondage. When I was old enough to drive, I fell deeper into the abyss of sin. In the summer months, my drinking escalated to a gallon of alcohol a day! When I could get it, marijuana was a daily vice as well. Pills and PCP would soon be added to the list of addictions. I still had a consciousness of God, but little or no conviction.

However, at 17 to 18 years old, the conviction of God began to grow! The draw of the Holy Spirit was accentuated by the love of my grandparents, aunts, and uncles who were saved. They showed me His love by saying things like, "Chris, you are going to preach some day!" "Chris, Jesus loves you!" Something was weighty about their words to me! I wouldn't immediately heed the Holy Spirit, but He was hot on my trail! I'm ashamed of my past! I would deceive, steal, and manipulate to support my drug and alcohol problems. I would go from house to house, party to party, not going home or even checking in with my family for nearly 90 days sometimes. I began to hate who I had become but repeated the vicious fixation over and over!

In all of this, I managed to stay in school and play sports. I was awarded a football scholarship to Maryville College. I was recruited as an outstanding tail back, punt and kick returner, and a cornerback. I was excited about it, but I had very little support of my accomplishment. I went to Maryville College with addictions and a broken heart due to all of the family drama! I was hoping to find some kind of peace, but due to having four practices a day to prepare for the upcoming season, my teammates and I popped pills to get through the aggressive schedule. The college had secured a summer job at Coca Cola Bottling Plant for some of the players to help with additional expenses while we were on campus. With the continued lack of guidance and support, I clung to the job, quit the football team, and surrendered my scholarship. I bounced around from friends and family homes but kept my job. I started getting high with more frequency. Somehow, I would make it to a bed, get sober or straight, and go to work the next day.

A local drug dealer worked with me at Coca Cola. When I would get to work, he would give me a pill, or on break or lunch we would smoke a joint to get through the day. We would become good friends! One morning I came to work, and my friend wasn't there. He missed a few days, and I found out that he was in the hospital facing some health issues. While in the hospital, he was visited by someone who shared the love of Jesus with him, and he received Christ into his life! When my buddy returned to work, his face was shining, and he was carrying a huge Bible! I hated him because he was different! Again, I heard the words from years ago, "Chris, Jesus loves you!" "Chris, God has a plan for your life." I was trying to make sense of this!

I settled back in at the little house trailer with Mom and my siblings on Self Hollow Road. On Saturdays, my buddy, who had just been saved, would drive up in an old wrecker, knock on the door, and ask me to go haul old junk cars for his side business. I would reluctantly go, many times hung over with a huge vacancy in my soul! My friend would have a hot biscuit and cup of coffee for me. Then, he would share those words again, "Chris, Jesus loves you!" "Chris, God has a plan for you!" Man, those words started to grip my heart! One weekend, he picked me up and said, "I have something for you to listen to." The night before, he had prayed all night for me to be delivered from my abusive lifestyle, and he had recorded the prayer. When I got in the wrecker, he hit play! I was hearing a recording of a man praying for me all night! Geez! My heart was so convicted! I now sensed a love that I had not known-the wonderful love of God! Eventually, one morning I went to work, clocked in, and began crying over what I had been experiencing along with the conviction of sin! I ran up to my friend and said, "I want what you got!" He told me to meet him outside in an old Coca-Cola warehouse at 9am. I went outside at 9am in November, 1982 and told my buddy I needed a life change! "I don't know how to do it," I said, and he said, "Pray." I said, "How do you do that?" He said, "Do you believe Jesus came to the world, died on a cross, and rose in three days from the dead?" I said, "Yes!" He said to me, "Are you sorry for all that you have done?" I said, "Yes!" He asked me to repeat a simple prayer, "Jesus save me, heal me, and forgive me!" And Jesus did! He forgave me! He delivered me that day from alcohol, drugs, and a lifestyle plagued with sin! A wind blew in that old warehouse that day; I heard the birds a-singing, the sun was shining, joy filled my soul, and perfect love healed me! Joy and love flooded from the depths of my being that day, and 36 years later still does!

Since that day, I have met the love of my life, sweet Rhonda, and together we have two children with loving spouses and two gorgeous granddaughters. I'm forever indebted to my wife's parents who have acted as my spiritual parents in this journey. Both of my parents have accepted Christ, which led to a sweeping revival through my entire immediate family! God turned my dysfunction into a wonderful, healthy life that I now enjoy. My wife and I have served in every imaginable assignment in the kingdom of God, and He has propelled our ministry from national to international seasons. We have served together for over 30 years of full time ministry. We live to continue to tell our story, right out of Self Hollow!

In this chapter, I dedicate all that I am to God; my beautiful, loving, and supportive wife, Rhonda; my two awesome kids, Christian and Gabriel; and their spouses, Jeff and Alexys (whom I love); and two grands Alexis and Arabelle (Poppy's heart).

CHRIS RENEAU serves as the Lead Pastor at The Meadow in Maryville, TN. He is married to his wife Rhonda and has two children and three grandchildren.

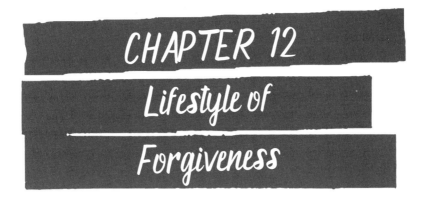

CHAPTER 12
Lifestyle of
Forgiveness

Pastor Nick Serban
FULL LIFE ASSEMBLY OF GOD

You don't have to be involved in ministry too many years to experience disappointment and pain. The up's and down's of emotion and stability are likened to a featured roller coaster, guaranteed to take you to the edge and back. Yes! That is what it has often felt like in my life.

But today, I sit and remind myself that "I WOULD DO IT ALL AGAIN." Foolish as it might seem. Do what you ask? I would and will keep loving, keep being vulnerable, keep putting myself out there in the midst of difficulties and life altering storms to navigate through. I would keep on forgiving, because I believe that God has not called us to anything less.

A few months ago, I agreed to a meet with a man who had deeply hurt and offended not only me, but the church I lead. I had purposed to move on and figured I'd never hear from him again. The conversation with this person started off with pleasantries and catching up. He proceeded to share that he was sorry for the past and wanted to return to the church and our friendship. You would think this was a sovereign WOW moment, but as if time stood still my brain began to kick into overdrive.

I listened and mentally started to dissect his statements. Was the tone of his voice sincere? Did he really think I would just let him off the hook, let him back in my life, let alone give him the opportunity to return to what he referred to as home, the local church? I could hear my early mentor in ministry speaking in my mind, "We must never strike the second blow, **because no provocation ever justifies an unchristian response.**" My flesh wanted justice, but my heart wanted grace to abound.

In the New Testament, grace means God's love in action towards men who deserved the opposite of love. Grace means God moving heaven and earth to save sinners who could not lift a finger to save themselves. Grace means God sending His only Son to descend into hell on the cross, so that we as guilty people might be reconciled to God and received into heaven.

My early studying and mentoring began to kick in. All the messages that I have sat through and the notes I had jotted in the front pages of my Bible. I remembered, "God chooses what we go through; we choose how we go through it!" as well as "Choose to lose when you could win!" This is what Jesus would do. I have taught my four sons that if someone has the heart and courage enough to say their sorry, look them in the eyes and verbalize to them I FORGIVE YOU.

Almost like a rehearsed reflex, pushing aside all my righteous indignation and justification, I responded. The next words out on my mouth were, "I forgive you, I let you off the hook, and you owe me nothing."

Forgiving and Forgetting. When we wrongly react to an offender, we are revealing various lacks of character. This character needs to be developed in us such as love, meekness, patience, faith, gentleness, self-control, etc. Even if we respond correctly to an offender, other qualities will have to be strengthened such as joy, peace, and goodness. When God allows someone to offend us, He is entrusting to us the responsibility to demonstrate Christ's love and presence to them. Who can stand in the presence of the Lord Jesus very long and remain the same person? Let's not BE SO OFFENDABLE.

In Philippians 2:13, Paul's prayer was that grace would be multiplied to every Christian. How then can we receive GRACE? BEING HUMBLED. God resists the proud but gives GRACE to the humble (James 4:6). Here is a key that leads to a peaceful long life. Give yourself the FREEDOM that FORGIVENESS gives you. Forgiveness is not a technique for self-improvement. Forgiveness is not just about you or about making yourself feel better. To forgive means to release from a claim, to cancel it, to wipe the record clean, to say the other no longer owes anything.

How do I fully forgive all who have offended me? The apostle Peter asked the question "How often will my brother sin again against me, and I forgive him? Till seven times?" (Matthew 18:21). The Jewish custom was to forgive three times? Peter must have been proud to present this offer to Jesus of more than three times, "How about seven times, Lord?"

Jesus answers with a parable in Matthew 18:23-34. A king takes account of his servants and finds one owing him 10,000 talents, about 9 million dollars. The king orders the servant and family to be sold for payments of the debt. The servant asks for patience, promising to pay his debt. The king was moved with compassion and frees him, completely forgiving the debt. The forgiven servant now goes out and finds one owing him 100 pence about $15.00. This servant threatens and demands immediate payment. The debtor begs for forgiveness. The forgiven servant "would not" forgive but puts the man in prison.

The king hears about the unforgiving servant and calls him "wicked." The servant that was forgiven of much failed to pass on his forgiveness to another. He, in turn, loses his forgiveness from the king, and is delivered to his creditors to pay back all he owes.

Jesus said the unforgiver will be turned over to the tormentors. Matthew 18:35 "This is how my heavenly Father will treat each of you unless you forgive your brother or sister from your heart." Jesus teaches in this parable our forgiveness of others is to be equal with God's forgiveness to us, limitless. We, who are forgiven by God of all, have no right or choice to think about forgiving. By right of our state of forgiveness in Christ, we are prohibited from harboring any bitterness, resentment or unforgiveness towards anyone. God will treat us the same way if we do not forgive. Forgiveness is not a feeling, but a choice and an act of our will.

Why is forgiveness a must? Hebrews 12:15 says, so that no bitter root grows up to cause trouble and defile many. Bitterness burns emotional energy. When this energy is exhausted, emotional depression results. Bitterness leads to doubt. Because of being hurt by people in the past, a bitter person cannot trust another. Bitterness causes a person to be hypersensitive to their own emotions, but insensitive to the feelings of others. A bitter person expects to be compensated for the hurts they have suffered. They feel the world owes them something.

Someone said that unforgiveness is the poison we drink while we wait for the other person to die. When we withhold forgiveness we forfeit so many things God want to do through our lives. See God's hand through your offender. God has allowed this offender into your life to teach you something. Ask Him how He is strengthening you through your experience. Totally forgive your offender. Forgive them of any hurt or damage regardless of your feelings. By an act of your will, choose to release them over to the Lord and be free from harboring any bad feelings.

FOUR WAYS TO FORGIVE
1. *Forgive because you feel like it, but you're probably not going to feel like it.*
2. *Forgive because the person who hurt you deserves it, although they really may not deserve it.*

3. *Forgive because you know that God won't hear prayers from an unforgiving heart.*
4. *Forgive because you know that God has forgiven you.*

Although our minds often race in the middle of circumstance, let's except the challenge to forgive immediately. Matthew 5:23-24 says, "Therefore, if you are offering your gift at the altar and there remember that your brother or sister has something against you, leave your gift there in front of the altar. First go and be reconciled to them; then come and offer your gift." Forgive totally. Ephesians 4:32 says, "Be kind and compassionate to one another, forgiving each other, just as in Christ God forgave you."

Forgiveness is: Forgiveness is an act of the will in which we choose not to hold someone's debt for the wrong they have done to us. Forgiveness is "letting go" of it's power over you! Mature followers of Christ don't allow other people's actions to dictate theirs. If they do, the offender and their negative emotions become their master instead of Christ. Corrie Ten Boom says, "Forgiveness is the key that unlocks the handcuffs of hatred and the door of resentment." The Bible shows us that forgiveness is the cancellation of a debt as if it never existed.

Jesus said we are to, "Forgive from our hearts." I believe we can walk, maintaining a heart that lives in the state of forgiveness at all times. Even before we are offended, our heart can be in the place of total forgiveness for any offender. When wronged, we can immediately release this offense to the Lord and continue to walk before God, free from any root of bitterness and unforgiveness.

This heart of forgiveness is the life of Jesus. Not only when He was on the cross, offended, but also in choosing Judas as one of the twelve disciples. Jesus knew three and a half years before His betrayal ever took place; He even predicted it, as did the Old Testament. Yet He picks this disciple and allows him full privileges during his ministry. This is a heart full of forgiveness before the offense ever takes place. God help us all to walk and maintain this heart of forgiveness at all times.

Let's refuse to let offenses stop us. Our offenses will either be our gravestone or our stepping-stone. Freely we have received and we must freely give. The man that I forgave came back into my life and returned to the church. Ironically, a few months later, he was offended again with another church member and would not forgive them. He has since left the church and ministry again. Today I sit and remind myself that "I WOULD DO IT ALL AGAIN". Foolish as it might seem. Do what you ask? I will keep loving, keep being vulnerable, keep putting myself out there in the midst of difficulties and life altering storms to navigate through. I will keep on forgiving because I believe that God has not called us to anything less.

NICK SERBAN III serves as the Lead Pastor of Full Life Assembly of God in Franklin, Tennessee and as the Executive Secretary for the Tennessee Assemblies of God Ministry Network. He has a passionate heart for missions and is committed to building the local church by helping people reach their full potential in Christ.

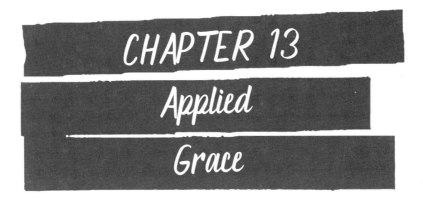

CHAPTER 13
Applied
Grace

Pastor Jeremy Songer
C1 CHURCH COLUMBIA

But by the grace of God I am what I am, and his grace toward me was not in vain. On the contrary, I worked harder than any of them, though it was not I, but the grace of God that is with me (1 Corinthians 15:10).

I Hurt Myself

Favor is a strange thing. When we have it with the right people things seem to work well in our life. The job promotions come, the opportunities are plentiful, and friends are everywhere. The opposite is true when we don't have favor. Influence is non-existent, people flee from our presence and rejection seems to slam every door of opportunity in our face.

Early in ministry I felt like it was an uphill battle to fulfill this call God had placed on my life. I put in more hours at the church, working hard to build anything I was given the opportunity to lead to success and pushing the people around me to do the same. The pastors I served under were very gracious to me. Allowing me to grow and overlooking my overzealous ambition. Unfortunately, my relationships suffered. Being task-driven I was focused on the destination much more than the journey. As I've grown as a disciple and pastor, I've discovered people are motivated much more by love than anxiety.

The favor we seek from people is natural. Everyone wants to be liked, admired, and valued. This desire to be in the good graces of people tips to an unhealthy level when we place the priority of human grace above God's grace. It's dangerous to desire human favor in excess. When I think of wanting favor in an unhealthy way, I'm reminded of grade school. I had just entered fourth grade in Mr. Thompson's class at Westside Elementary in the little northern Georgia town where I was raised. There was a blonde girl named Kari in my class that had caught my eye. I decided I would make my intentions to her known. My grandmother had a cheap knock off piece of jewelry she had discarded. Before it was tossed I had what I thought was an incredible idea. I would take this piece of junk jewelry to her and ask her to be my girl. There was one small complication with all of this. She had a boyfriend named Justin in sixth grade. He was a foot taller than me and his bicep muscles looked to be the size of my head. I told one of my friends what I was going to do. To my demise this friend wasn't so loyal. He went to Justin and told him my plan. After school as I was walking to the bus, Justin cut me off in the hallway. Before I could run he had slammed me into the snack machine and roughed me up good. I never even told her I liked her. Epic fail. In all my desire to have the beginnings of a fairy-tale romance I hadn't considered the reality that she was committed to someone else and the consequences of intruding on that commitment.

Many times, we find ourselves in positions of pain when we don't properly count the cost and access the consequences of our decisions. Each choice, each move comes with rewards or penalties. The grace God gives us through Jesus is not just a get-out-of-our beating because we step over the line opportunity, it's an invitation to understand His favor is much more valuable than any human affection. My work hasn't earned His grace toward me, if anything its in-spite of the things I've done that He loves me. The incredible thing that goes counterintuitive to human thinking is that this favor isn't a license to do what we want, but a release to live out Gods purpose for our lives. It takes away the victim tag so many of us hold onto so tightly as our primary identity. You may feel too fat or skinny, over-educated, or uneducated, attractive, or unattractive.

"You made all the delicate, inner parts of my body and knit me together in my mother's womb. Thank you for making me so wonderfully complex! Your workmanship is marvelous—how well I know it" (Psalms 139:13-14).

Recently, I had a revelation from this passage. The Psalmist David details how God sees him and then he ends the 14th verse with, "How well I know it." This is the David that failed God, missed opportunities to instruct his children, had an affair and had the husband of his mistress killed. He says "Your workmanship is marvelous" speaking of himself. He didn't argue with how God saw him. There isn't a list in the passage of how God messed up with David or how if David's dad Jesse would have been more loving he would've known how to be a better dad, king, or husband. There is no blame in Psalm 139, only praise because of the Creator's amazing work. How easy is it for us to forget that God has blessed us with eyes to see, ears to hear, hands to feel, and a mind to understand? It is God's great mercy that formed us, knowing we would fail Him repeatedly. Our failure doesn't diminish his love for us. It comes with consequences but one of those consequences, is never a loss of His love toward us.

I am no Orphan

Feeling the insufficiency of who we are is one of the primary indicators of our need for God. Unfortunately, the desire to prove our self-worth can lead to destructive habits if healing is not sought in scripture, wise counsel, and prayer. My desire to prove myself in ministry was derived from my insecurity. The internal belief that people didn't like me and, truth be told, I didn't like me. The way I looked, sounded, or any number of other areas of my life. I was raised by a Godly dad and mom but no matter who our parents are we are born into a broken world. Images of who we are can come from TV, Music, and people's opinions. I firmly believed God's grace was powerful to save people. My mind knew God loved me but secretly my heart believed I was a disappointment to my family, church and yes to God. The harder I worked the more I felt rejected. The more I rested the more anxious I became. The answer for my condition came from a perspective shift on grace. It wasn't that God was giving me a license to live how I wanted but an authority to live how He intended. I wasn't working from defeat or loss but from victory. My deficiency was erased at the cross. I'm fully accepted as His son. My Father says I'm worthy, so I am worthy.

What now

On February 3, 2015, my first wife died of breast cancer two days shy of our son's first birthday. The year leading up to this tragedy was the most challenging year of our lives. On February 2nd, we'd just completed a major remodel of our 20,000-square foot facility at the church we pastored. The grand opening was incredible. We broke attendance records. We'd come a long way from the fourteen attendees we started with in the summer of 2010. My wife, Janna, was pregnant with our second child (Joseph). He was due to be born soon. She had begun experiencing severe pain in her back. As the pregnancy progressed it got worse. She was nearly bed ridden the couple of weeks leading up to this day. That evening after the grand opening we had a Super Bowl party scheduled. Our daughter Josie was three and Janna was hurting too bad to care for her, so I took Josie with me to the party. Just a few moments into the party Janna calls me and says, "I think my water broke". I dropped everything at the church and took our daughter to our admin assistants house and took Janna to the hospital. Labor was unusually painless. On February 3rd, early in the morning, Joseph Luke Songer a healthy baby boy was born, though our joy was short lived. Janna, moments after the birth, collapsed unable to walk or move her legs, waist or left hand. They began running test to determine the cause. The first thought was maybe a side effect from the epidural. They began running tests. The next day I went home to spend some time with our daughter and returned with breakfast. As I walked in the room one of our deacon's wives was in tears and sweet Janna was also. They asked me to sit down they had to talk to me about what was going on. The Doctor came in and had informed them that tumors lined her spine and cancer was in her breast and on her liver. Numbness came over my body and I began to cry uncontrollably. I wept. So many thoughts ran through my mind. "This can't be she's so faithful to you God. Our babies need their mom. Please Lord no!" We believed God for a miracle. We prayed, fasted, and trusted the Lord. Over the next year I became a care taker for Janna while also being a dad to a newborn and a toddler. A lot of people stepped up in our lives and helped us.

On February 3rd, 2015 I felt like, What was the point of this! I remember weeping over Janna's lifeless body and crying out to God I don't know why, but I trust you.

The next few months were a blur for me. Although I can remember sitting in the District Council for the Assemblies of God (the fellowship we are a part of) the April following Janna's passing, I really in my heart had decided I couldn't keep pastoring. The speaker for that session was Choco DeJesus. He talked about feeling the gaps in our community. He then told us about a conference for pastors and church leaders. I heard the Holy Spirit speak deep within me to go to that conference and bring three people with me. The Lord restored me at the conference and it was a turning point for my healing. Since then I've remarried and the Lord has done an incredible work of restoration in our family. After Job's trial, God blesses him with twice what he'd lost. The Lord is faithful to reward our faithfulness.

It has been the Lord's grace that has sustained me in every season of my life. His grace requires us to trust Him for it to be affective in our lives. We must stop believing the lies the enemy tells us. God isn't punishing you with your circumstances and situations. He is using the trials of life to refine us and make us better.

Don't stay stuck. As a kid, when a metal door would get stuck my dad would spray WD-40 on it and the door would work again. Grace is like the spiritual WD-40 of our lives, when we apply it to the right places it will get us unstuck. The question isn't, does God want to make us better. The question is, do we really want to be better?

We can make progress or we can make excuses, but we can't do both. Responsibility for self-development must be the primary focus of utilizing the grace God has provided each of us. I doubled down on reading the Word, spiritually uplifting books and materials. I spent intentional time in prayer and worship. God can and will deliver you from trouble. Whether you make mistakes or life just happens to you. Grace is the ability to renew the trust you may have lost. Your trust in God will restore your hope in life. I hope the words I've shared have encouraged you.

JEREMY SONGER is the Lead Pastor of C1.Church in Columbia, Tennessee. Husband of a world changer, Father of two great kids, Friend of God & Servant of the least of them.